"From Word to Image *is one of the most invaluable film guid*[...]*than a year of film school. The visualization process of mo*[...]*with startling clarity and intelligence. Marcie Begleiter is the go-to teacher for learning the concepts and techniques behind creating a visual script.*"

> —Bill Condon, Director, *Dreamgirls, Kinsey, Gods and Monsters*

"*Marcie Begleiter is the person to explain, to give perspective, and to examine the art and craft of storyboarding.* From Word to Image *continues her teaching with examples, color photos, and very practical filmmaking information. I have experienced firsthand the impact her work has had on filmmakers. Her contribution to AFI's Directing Workshop for Women has influenced award-winning directors who have gone on to direct features* (College)*, television* (Mad Men)*, and shorts* (Mother)*.*"

> —Joe Petricca, Executive Vice Dean, AFI Conservatory

"From Word to Image *provides a great foundation for the communication of visual concepts for moving imagery. Through this book Marcie provides the essential language for collaboration in the visual storytelling process. In essence, she has sharpened your pencils and provided the perfect page for you to spill out your ideas and have them understood.*"

> —Steve Martino, Blue Sky Studios; Director, *Horton Hears a Who*;
> Art Director, *Robots*

"From Word to Image *offers a rare and inspiring clarity about the role of visual preparation within the many forms of 'moving' entertainment. Enhanced by an impressive variety of iconic guest perspectives and material on the use of color in storytelling, the new edition provides much more than a typical instructional text; it functions as career guidance on a world-class level.*"

> —Robert Peterson, Chair of Graduate Broadcast Cinema,
> Art Center College of Design

"*The creation of art for the 21st century and its use in storytelling are undergoing radical philosophical changes.* From Word to Image *is targeted at that discussion's cutting edge and shows how the practice is shaping up. It is a must-read for anyone involved in this process.*"

> —Dan Forcey, Vice President, Content Development, Platinum Studios

"*Storyboarding is a powerful tool, and the second edition of this classic text continues in the well-known tradition of Begleiter's work.* From Word to Image *has brought increased clarity to my work—formerly as a director and writer, currently as a producer—by expanding my ability to visualize as well as communicate with collaborators. Highly recommended for directors, writers, cameramen, producers, and designers alike.*"

> —Rita Nasser, Executive Producer, Fiction Film, German Public Television, ZDF

"*Marcie was my storyboarding mentor at the American Film Institute when I received a grant from the Directing Workshop for Women in 1999. Because of the skills I learned in her class, I storyboarded my first short film, which was incredibly helpful in commu-*nicating with my crew... The 2nd Edition of From Word to Image, *with its new chapter on color, has been remarkably valuable as I plan my future projects, and has helped me visualize my shots in a way that no lecture ever could.*"

> —Lily Mariye, Director, *The Shangri-la Café*; Actor, *ER*

"If you are in the business of filmmaking as director, production designer, or story-boarder, the contents of From Word to Image *should be engraved on the inside of your eyelids. Begleiter's book is accessible, knowledgeable, and sophisticated in presentation. Its blend of art, technical expertise, and personal experience is authoritative and quite exceptional."*

—Elaine Masden, Emmy Award-winning documentary Director and Author

"In today's fast-paced, digitally-driven multimedia world, many basic skills in design, planning, and storytelling are quickly fading. Too often I work with young filmmakers who don't know the history of their craft; they don't know the basics of photography, camera choreography, lighting, staging a scene, or story structure. From Word to Image *is the definitive guide to the essential tools in visual storytelling. This book should be required reading for all who are serious about making a career in the visual arts and filmmaking."*

—Richard Winn Taylor II, 30-year member of the DGA; Effects Director, *Tron*; Co-Creative Director, yU+Co

"Begleiter has given the subject its own place in the sun through this groundbreaking practical guide and historic companion."

—*Directors Guild Magazine*

"Begleiter's book is very thorough; 18 years of experience in the motion-picture industry have given her the tools to illustrate complex concepts with great visual immediacy."

—*American Cinematographer Magazine*

"A wonderfully logical book about a precise tool to use in an illogical medium. Marcie Begleiter's process is a visual and organizational assist to any filmmaker trying to shift from story in words to story in moving image."

—Joan Tewkesbury, Screenwriter, *Nashville*; Director, *Felicity*

"So often as writers, we concentrate on words: which words sound good, how they flow, how they work together on the page. But From Word to Image *reminds us that as TV and film writers, our words are simply conduits to pictures... and Begleiter's book helps us think about those pictures in practical new ways. I'd recommend this book not only to directors, DPs, and storyboard artists, but to any artist who uses words to bring pictures to life, including writers."*

—Chad Gervich, TV Writer/Producer, *Wipeout*; Author, *Small Screen, Big Picture: A Writer's Guide to the TV Business*

"As someone who has always been interested in the previsualization and storyboarding process, I found From Word to Image *truly appealing. Step-by-step guides walk the reader through storyboard techniques, script breakdown, shot lists, how to express camera angles, and much more — all wonderfully illustrated by examples. I highly recommend this book to anyone who wants to get into storyboarding or improve their skills."*

—Mark Sickle, Managing Editor, *The Independent Source Magazine*

from word to image

to image

storyboarding and the filmmaking process

2nd edition

MARCIE BEGLEITER

Published by Michael Wiese Productions
3940 Laurel Canyon Blvd. # 1111
Studio City, CA 91604
tel. 818.379.8799
fax 818.986.3408
mw@mwp.com
www.mwp.com

Cover Design: MWP
Interior Book Design: Gina Mansfield Design
Editor: Linda Norlen

Printed by Sheridan Books, Ann Arbor, Michigan
Manufactured in the United States of America

Library of Congress Cataloging-in-Publication Data

Begleiter, Marcie,
 From word to image : storyboarding and the filmmaking process / by Marcie
Begleiter. -- 2nd ed.
     p. cm.
Includes bibliographical references.
 ISBN 978-1-932907-67-4
1. Storyboards. 2. Commercial art--Technique. I. Title.
 NC1002.S85B44 2010
 791.4302'3--dc22
                          2009029579

TABLE OF CONTENTS

for
Jeff and Zachary

"First, I storyboarded it."

There have been many people who have helped in the research, writing, and editing of this book. I would like to thank the librarians at the film archives of UCLA, USC, and AFI; Barbara Hall, Scott Curtis, and others at the Margaret Herrick Library of the Academy of Motion Pictures Arts and Sciences; and the Museum of Modern Art for their help in tracking down many of the storyboard examples in this volume. In addition, Helen Cohen and the Cecil B. DeMille Estate were very gracious in allowing me to photograph their collection. Many of the quotes and interviews in the book have been transcribed from interviews conducted in 1999. I want to extend thanks to Harold and Lillian Michelson, Robert Boyle, Robert Wise, Gene Allen, John Jensen, Richard Hoover, Joe Musso, John Mann, Frank Gladstone, Ron Gress, and John Coven for their time and cooperation.

I would also like to thank the estate of Alfred Hitchcock and Leland H. Faust for his help in securing the rights to reproduce material from the collection, which is held by the Margaret Herrick Library. George Roy Hill has generously allowed us to reproduce his drawings and Edwin Brown was most helpful in helping to secure that release. The chapter on job opportunities was enhanced by the comments of Cynthia Paskos and Gina Mandela of Local 790 and the agents Mark Miller and Philip Mittel.

A project this size is rarely accomplished solo and I'd like to express thanks to Gary Perkovac and Peter Carpenter for their aid with the illustrations, Channee Edwards for helping to round up the clearances and Vee Vitanza, David Neeham, and Grant Powell for their work on the appendix of websites.

The crew at Michael Wiese Productions has been a support all along the way. I especially want to thank Michael for suggesting this project and not taking no for an answer. Lisa Wexton has given me editorial as well as moral support throughout; Milena Albert and Ken Lee have helped to keep the project well organized and on deadline. B. J. Markel helped to add the final polish.

A word also to Chris Craig and his team at the AFI Professional Training Division for the long-term support of my work and their willingness to make creative leaps in the service of film education. Also, Bob Peterson, the chairman of the film department at Art Center College of Design, has helped to support and develop the classes from which this book grows. The Faculty Council at Art Center supported the book with a generous grant that helped to pay for the image clearances. And last, but certainly not least, I want to thank Anita

Hyshiver for her many months of advice and insights into this mysterious process of bringing forth a book where nothing stood before.

And for the second edition, I'd like to add my thanks to Richard Taylor, Dan Forcey, and Steve Martino for their thoughtful interviews (conducted in 2008) as well as Diane Russell for her help in updating the appendices. Also many thanks to Linda Norlen for her thoughtful help in editing the text and suggestions regarding graphic design. The material on color has been developed in coursework at both Art Center College of Design and the Otis College of Art and Design.

In the winter of 1984 I found myself on a film set on Cape Cod. A scenic design company had sent me to paint sets for a film that was about to shoot in Provincetown, Massachusetts. I was a struggling artist, showing sporadically in the art galleries of Boston and taking on theater design and craft gigs to pay my studio rent.

One day while hanging out on top of a ladder I overheard a conversation between the director and the production office back in Los Angeles. He was vigorously requesting that a storyboard artist be sent out to the set. The crew was slated to start shooting in two weeks, and there were some key scenes that needed to be worked out. I could only hear one side of the conversation, but it was clear that his need was great and yet they were not about to spend the money to fly someone out to Massachusetts.

I didn't know what a storyboard was, but I did know that it had something to do with drawing, and drawing was something I knew about. At dinner that evening I sat next to the production designer thinking about how I would broach the subject, when he turned to me and said, "I want you to know that you can ask me anything." For a second I was shocked, but I recovered enough to take a deep breath and leap into my proposal that the production hire me to work on the storyboards.

He looked surprised and let out a groan, "Oh, no. We just hired someone this afternoon. Too bad, I would have liked to give you a chance. We'll have to catch you on the next one." I was distraught. If only I'd spoken up sooner, I might have been able to stay with the crew and get some great experience. I went back to my hotel room that night and packed my bag. I was due to return to Boston the next morning.

At 6 a.m. the phone rang. I groggily answered it and heard a chipper voice declare, "If you can get over here in 20 minutes with a sharpened pencil, we'll give you a shot. The other artist just backed out." I jumped into my clothes and ran over to the production office. The designer told me that they were about to leave on an all-day location scout and I was to stick close to the director, not ask too many questions, and take notes on everything he said about camera positioning, blocking, and composition.

For the next fourteen hours I dutifully followed the many-headed beast that a film crew tends to resemble. I wrote and listened and tried to make sense out of the new vocabulary that was being tossed about. At the end of the day I went back to my room both elated and exhausted. It was the beginning of two months on location and fourteen years of work and study in the art and business of film.

I moved to Los Angeles after finishing the film in the Cape and eventually expanded my experience to include set decoration and art direction. But I always returned to preproduction visualization. I storyboarded, helped directors create shot lists and overhead diagrams, and generally acted as a visual assistant on many feature film and television projects.

In 1990 I was invited to teach a seminar on storyboarding at the American Film Institute. I created a weekend workshop based on my experiences working with first-time directors. These men and women often came to directing through writing and were much less comfortable communicating about the visual aspects of the medium than they were about the narrative. I set out to make visual communication accessible to those filmmakers who felt they had no "talent" for it.

From the beginning, the workshop achieved a popularity neither AFI nor I had anticipated. I added private workshops, held each month at a local hotel. Eventually I was asked to join the film faculty at Art Center College of Design in Pasadena, California. My experience there working with student filmmakers allowed me to develop a curriculum that encompasses many aspects of previsualization for film, including color theory, composition, storyboarding, and narrative structure as it applies to constructing the frame.

This book is an extension of the work that has come out of those classes as well as others I have given at the Director's Guild of America, the University of Southern California, and the International Film School in Cologne, Germany. It has brought me great joy to introduce and expand upon the aesthetic as well as the technical aspects of visualization for film. I hope that the information contained in this volume will be of some use to you in your projects, whether they be for the classic media of film and television or the many varieties of new media (CD-ROMs, the Internet, etc.) that take us beyond linear structure.

When *From Word to Image* was released on September 12, 2001, the world was entering a new era. Since that time our culture, media, and the methods we use to express ourselves have changed with a speed that is impressive and at times hard to track.

I decided to write an expanded edition of what has become a widely used text about visualization in order to support new research into narrative image making. Simply said, we are telling thousands of stories through media that did not even exist eight short years ago. On the home front, entry-level HD recorders mean that even beginning students have access to low-cost, professional-quality image making. GarageBand offers music studio features to score your project and YouTube affords access to a worldwide audience. Never have so many visual storytellers been able to say so much with so little to so many.

On the professional front, there has been significant movement on screens large and small. Digital projection for feature films is quickly becoming the norm, especially for films that have been created using digital technology. Analogue signals for broadcast television are scheduled to be turned off in 2009, and this event will push our culture even further down the digital road. And video gaming has become a larger industry than film, judging by capital investment and money spent on the ever-growing library of titles.

All of this activity means that the ability to become a content creator has shifted, in a significant manner, from the classic centralization of studio production to alternative systems sited in home offices, media classrooms, and the streets.

That being the case, a comprehensive chapter on the use of color seemed in line with the expanded reach of the industry as well as the goals of this text. The pervasive use of color in most contemporary projects by filmmakers and other graphic storytellers leads to an expanded conversation about the narrative possibilities of this nonverbal area of communication. Through a combination of historical research and practical experience, this material offers an approach to the analysis of existing material as well as defining a scope of inquiry for making informed decisions on projects in process.

In thinking about new content for this edition, I focused on working with industry professionals who are currently developing projects in live action, digital animation, and online media that offer cross-platform projects — such as the Platinum Studio model of film/comic books/online community content — interesting case studies in interdisciplinary processes and distribution.

So inside you will find new material presented in the form of case studies on pre-viz for animation, game design, and multi-platform content development. The appendices are full of new DVD titles, which include design-based supplementary content such as storyboards, animatics, concept illustrations, and scene-to-storyboard comparisons. The website list has been updated and the bibliography has some exciting new additions as well.

I'd also like to thank some people who have taken the time to be interviewed and read the manuscript as it developed. Richard Taylor, the awesomely talented cinematics director of Electronic Arts (EA); Dan Forcey, VP of content development at Platinum Studios; and Steve Martino, director of the animated feature *Horton Hears a Who* and art director of *Robots*.

My intention with this new material is to offer both an appreciation of a developing aesthetic as well as information on new processes and techniques. The information is intended to support both educational as well as professional projects and I hope it will find a place on your bookshelf among other words and images that seek to support a healthy and playful creative process.

[*Lifeboat*, 1944]

This book is intended for filmmakers such as directors, writers, designers, and cinematographers as well as those in the related fields of art and design who would like to transfer their skills to a new medium. Anyone working in either the traditional arts of film and television or those exploring the new domains of digital video, CD-ROMs, and the Internet will find ideas and techniques that will expand their communication skills.

THE DETAILS

The first portion of the book will focus on detailing a series of techniques that will enhance your ability to communicate about the visual aspects of storytelling. Breaking down a script into shot sequences, understanding the use of different camera moves and angles, as well as how to express your choices to your collaborators are covered with multiple examples and exercises at the end of each chapter. In the second section (Chapters 6–10) the material covers more aesthetic issues, such as the use of composition and color and their use in building visual narrative. The last chapters touch on skill development for readers who are relatively new to image making. And

> "I think one of the biggest problems that we have in our business is the inability of people to visualize. Imagine a composer sitting down with a blank music sheet in front of him, and a full orchestra. 'Flute, give me a note if you please. Yes, thank you very much,' and he writes it down. It's the same thing, but a man can compose music directly on paper and what's the result? It comes out as gorgeous sounds. The visual, to me, is a vital element in this work. I don't think it is studied enough."
>
> — Alfred Hitchcock
> *Directing the Film*

then, finishing the volume, you'll find appendices on current computer applications that can help with pre-viz, a list of DVDs that have supplemental tracks on storyboarding and related art, as well as lists of websites and books that cover allied topics.

More specifically, this book has been broken down into chapters on production, history of the craft, creating a visual shot list, overhead diagramming, and drawing. In addition, one chapter offers ideas about how to express camera movement with the use of frames extended beyond their usual aspect ratio. Another covers the basics of composition with an emphasis on narrative. There is also an illustrated glossary that links words, images, and diagrams for some of the most commonly used terminology in film and video production.

Preproduction visualization is an exciting, demanding process that begins in your imagination and ends with concrete documents that describe your project with imagery. This book will supply you with the tools you need to communicate the visual aspects of your work. You do not need to be an accomplished artist or even feel comfortable about drawing to accomplish this task. While you are learning some simple techniques, this book will lead you on a journey to visual awareness.

Each chapter covers a different aspect of visual communication and how it relates to film and video preproduction. Creating a visually specific shot list, developing an overhead diagram, and expressing your vision through the simple sketching of perspective and figures will be explored in detail. In addition, there are numerous examples of storyboards and other preproduction documents from the history of film and television. The material that is presented strives to be both accessible to the beginner and challenging to the professional.

WHY STORYBOARD?

Film and video are highly collaborative media. Most projects depend on the input and cooperation of dozens, if not hundreds, of coworkers. In order for the production to work smoothly, there needs to be a method to communicate about the numerous decisions that must be made by each department and coordinated by the director and his or her senior staff. The storyboard and its related documents — the shot list and the overhead diagram — are essential tools for communicating visual ideas to the entire crew.

Storyboarding involves logistical as well as aesthetic considerations. Time is money, and time spent planning during preproduction is much cheaper than time spent while the cameras are rolling. Any decisions that can be made

[*Quo Vadis*, 1951]
Director: Mervyn LeRoy

prior to principal photography are less expensive decisions than those made on the set. Whether it is a decision regarding the movement of the camera or the blocking of the characters, storyboarding can make your choices clearer from the camera's point of view. From establishing the number of setups needed for a stunt or prioritizing your needs for a special effects shot, preproduction visualization brings the crew closer to a unified purpose.

A film or video project is rarely shot without a script. And, just as a screenplay is the script for the narrative of a story, the storyboard is the visual script. Storyboards allow the director time and space to translate the dialogue and action of the screenplay into the language of imagery. When a director first begins the process of visualizing the script, he or she is faced with an unbroken narrative of story line. Contemporary screenwriting style avoids describing camera angles or visual transitions and mainly sticks to describing action and expressing dialogue. The overhead diagram, shot list, and storyboard images are often the first time that the script is translated into imagery. The words of the script may be poetic, but the storyboard is a concrete realization of that poetry into space and time.

> "Good pre-planning is probably the most important thing, if you want to make a picture within a reasonable budget. If you don't want to waste money, it is very, very important to plan it out. I make little thumbnail sketches all along, and it works. This comes from the animation technique that... taught me to make storyboards."
>
> — George Pal
> *Directing the Film*
> Director: *The Time Machine,* dozens of animated shorts

THE APPROACH

Storyboarding is often thought of as imagery: minimal sketches that illustrate what the camera will see and how it will move. Our approach will encompass a larger task through the use of a three-tiered document made up of:

> **Text** (the script and shot list)

> **Diagrams** (overhead schematics)

> **Images** (drawings, photos, computer graphic imagery)

This trilogy of form takes into consideration that the information will be accessible to all manner of minds. Everyone sees things differently. Imagery is concrete; it has a visible connection to the object it signifies. Show a picture of a chair to people unfamiliar with the object and they'll be able to find it in a room immediately. But use the word with people who don't speak English and they won't understand what you're talking about. Words are abstract and leave lots of room open for interpretation. A "follow-shot" of a character can be set up from any number of angles and move in many different ways. We need a language that is broad enough for everyone to understand.

In some ways, the diagram is the best of both worlds. It is both concrete and abstract. It can show where the actors are in relation to the settings and the movement of characters and cameras. Symbols such as arrows and boxes with angles attached can be used to represent blocking and camera positions. The diagram may be the most powerful document of the trilogy, as it can express a large amount of information in a minimal structure.

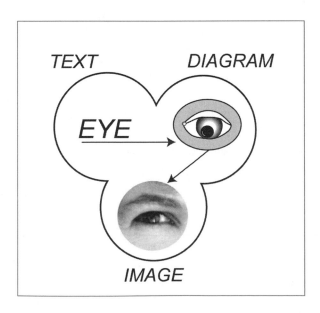

The connection of these three documents — the image (a drawing or photo-based representation), text (the shot list), and diagram (an overhead of the set with camera positions and character blocking) — assures that anyone reading the preproduction material will get the message. Translating the information into these three languages guarantees that you will be understood.

[*Ivan the Terrible*, 1944]
Drawing: Sergei Eisenstein

Through examples culled from the history of film and the writings and interviews of filmmakers, we will explore the ideas — both in words and images — that have influenced the process of envisioning a work and communicating that vision to one's collaborators.

As you work through the information in the book, you may find some of it familiar, while other sections challenge your abilities. Do not be intimidated by the new material. If you're accustomed to dealing with the world on a verbal level, then visual expression will be a stretch. That's OK — muscles that haven't been used for a long time may ache as they are exercised again.

THE FIVE "A"S

The five areas covered in the book will significantly affect the way you think about and express yourself regarding visual thought:

> **Assessment** of the script's narrative structure and the translation of story content to visual detail. The conscious use of composition and color can be a powerful storytelling tool. You rarely need to tell the audience what you can show them.

> **Ability** to express vision. Once you have the image in your mind's eye, you need the skill to be able to project and render it onto paper.

> **Attention** to the frame. The perimeters of our visual awareness are defined by the shape and the content of the frame. The chapters on aspect ratio, extended framing, and composition will focus attention in this area.

> **Awareness** of movement. There are two dynamics to this equation: movement of the frame (the camera) and movement inside the frame (the characters and the props).

> **Agreement** between text and image. The shot list and the images that represent its visual content must point to the same decisions. For example, if the shot list says to pan from a profile close-up to an American shot of another character, the image must show that move, that scale, that angle.

HOW TO USE THIS BOOK

A final word about the way to use this book: The chapters have been arranged to flow from general information to the specifics of technique. You may want to skim all the chapters briefly and then come back for a closer look once you have a feeling for the structure. Or you can start at the beginning and work your way through each section. Along the way, the words of various directors, designers, illustrators, and other visual thinkers are sprinkled throughout the text to give alternate points of view on the process of visualization.

However you approach the work, remember that you are teaching your mind and your body to see and communicate in a new way. This can be frustrating as well as rewarding. Allow yourself to fail and soon you will find yourself succeeding at a new level of ability. There is often a breakdown before a breakthrough. You may be surprised by the speed of your progress.

[*Destination Tokyo*, 1943]
Director: Delmer Daves

HERE COMES THE MASERATI

Occasionally I have been asked to create artworks for characters who are painters. This artist-for-hire position can be a good fill-in for the quiet times between features. I've done nudes for Jennifer Jason Leigh and landscapes for Sally Field. Murals for Korean, Hispanic, and Japanese painters. And once, an entire outdoor art fair.

The scene called for a group of paintings that had been produced by various artists, like you would see in a group show. The challenge was that this art show was to have an unwanted guest — a fiery red Maserati that was to speed through the show, scattering canvases in its wake. Most rental houses would look unkindly at treating their artwork in this manner.

The art director asked me to create a total of 42 works in six different styles. The scene was scheduled to be shot the next week. Forty-two paintings in six days. The art department dropped off the blank canvases on Monday morning and I sat staring at them for a good long while. I realized what I had committed to and was feeling like being committed. Then I decided to approach it like a storyboard assignment. My usual method is to sit down and write up a shot list, then rough out all the drawings in the morning, spending only 5-7 minutes on each image. Then after lunch, I'll go back into them and tighten up the drawing, ink them, and add light and shadows.

I started out by making a list of the six different artists' styles I would attempt to represent. I did faux O'Keeffes, fake Dalis, and phony Cassatts, among others. Then I spent an hour priming the canvases with a few base colors. When that dried, each got a one-hour treatment in the artist style of the day. They were not good paintings, but they passed at a distance, and that was the idea.

The canvases were shipped off to the art fair, and I was invited to be on site when the Maserati made its way through the easels. It was delicious fun. Most of the paintings were damaged or destroyed during the several takes needed to shoot the scene. I left as the crew was shoveling the remains into a dumpster. It's best not to get attached to the work.

I thought nothing of their fate until years later, when I arrived for an interview at the production offices of the company that had made the film. I looked up as I walked into the office and there were the familiar fakes that I had whipped out in my little West L.A. studio. Someone had rescued the least damaged ones and taken them back to the art department. They had been circulating for years on the walls of the floating production offices. From one show to the next, they had become part of an unofficial rotating library of art.

[*My Fair Lady*, 1964]
Director: George Cukor

What is a storyboard? The answer may seem self-evident, but the reality is more complex and interesting than just simple, framed drawings. This chapter will cover the definition of storyboards and how they are used in different preproduction processes. Following the journalist's guideline of covering "the five W's" of a story, the information is broken down into **what**, **why**, **who**, **when**, and **where**. These short essays deal with the physical properties of the storyboard — who develops it and who gets to see it down the line, how to prioritize the script in terms of which scenes require boarding first, and when the process usually takes place within the schedule of production.

"If George Cukor wanted me to do sketches and work with the cameraman on getting the shots set up, he would do it. On *My Fair Lady* that's the way he had me working with him. That's just the relationship between the director and his production designer. It was ideal. Cukor was a big enough person so that he never felt it was taking anything away from him. His attitude was 'If I can hire him, I can fire him. And if I can fire him I don't worry about him.' "
    —Gene Allen
        Production designer:
        My Fair Lady

What kinds of storyboards are used in the various entertainment industries? There is more than one kind of storyboard, and each one has its own style as well as different types of content. This section covers the general attributes of these documents as well as the varied uses they have in filmmaking, television production, commercials, and interactive media.

Why do we use storyboards in preproduction? The dividing line between preproduction and production is the beginning of principal photography. Before the crew and cast are present, making visual decisions can be done in a quieter, more contemplative environment. Once the "troops" arrive, the decision-making can turn more logistic than aesthetic. The "why" of storyboarding concerns itself with both of these factors.

Who creates the storyboard and its related documents? This part of the chapter deals with which crewmembers are included in the process of creating the visual script as well as who receives the board if the director chooses to circulate it to the crew.

Where and **when** is the storyboard created? This section covers the use of locations, set designs, and scheduling when working on preproduction visualization. The chapter will also include an outline for the storyboard conference — usually a meeting between the director and an illustrator or art director — and how to best use the time to visualize the film frame.

The preproduction process is as varied as the people who work within it. Take this information as it is intended — as a general map of the preproduction process, which changes with each shift of perspective.

FYI: A WORD ON ORDER

You may notice that this list of W's does not follow the proscribed order of who, what, where, when, why. That is because in production, you really need to understand what the process is before you determine who is going to be a part of it and when it is going to happen.

> **what**
> **why**
> **who**
> **when**
> **where**

[*The Greatest Show on Earth*, 1952]
Director: Cecil B. DeMille
Drawing: John Jensen

WHAT IS A STORYBOARD?

The use of the storyboard, as well as the shot list and overhead diagram, is widespread in many fields of the entertainment industry. Commercials, industrial films, CD-ROMs, and websites all use some form of storyboarding to help plan out the relationship of images to other aspects of the project.

Different media and the various artists and technicians who work in them have different needs and use different types of boards. The following pages will plot out basic styles and the uses that storyboards have within the various industries.

"*The Greatest Show on Earth* didn't have a script or anything at the time I met DeMille. But he liked to see visualizations of things. He said, 'I want you to go and travel with the circus and sketch everything you think looks interesting.' So I traveled with the circus and lived with them on the circus train. I stayed with them a couple of months. And later on, after I'd been sketching up these scenes a while, he'd have the writers write the story around these sketches."

— John Jensen
    Illustrator: *The Greatest Show on Earth*

"In silent films we didn't have all the words to explain everything; we thought in terms of symbols, graphic arrangements, or possibilities. We were trained in these terms. When you had to explain something you didn't think, 'What's the exact word for this? The exact phrase or sentence?' You just thought, 'What's the picture, the symbol?' "

—King Vidor
Directing the Film
Director: *The Crowd,*
Our Daily Bread

Storyboards can be referred to as:

> **Editorial Storyboards**

> **Key Frames**

> **Production Illustrations**

> **Commercial Boards**

EDITORIAL STORYBOARDING

> Plots out the editorial sequencing (how the shots will be edited, not the order of shooting)

> Reflects the creative concepts of the Director

> 8-1/2" by 11" format, usually for one to four frames per page

> Black and white

> Quick sketch

There are a few types of storyboards, but we will only cover one of these in detail in this book. The film and television industries use the Editorial method to give visual expression to the flow of edited sequences from the screenplay. These images are most often characterized by quick black-and-white sketches and can be simple line drawings or complex renderings of light and shadow.

The editorial storyboard is a Xerox art form in the sense that in most cases, the crew rarely works off the original storyboards. Instead, photocopies are made of the originals and then distributed to the crew. The storyboards need to be high contrast so they will reproduce well, so black-and-white storyboards are standard. In special circumstances, a Saturday matinee-type movie such as *Indiana Jones and the Raiders of the Lost Ark* will be rendered in color. High-style productions can benefit from adding color in the early stages of preproduction visualization, and obviously, movies with that kind of budget can afford the luxury of this more time-demanding process. What's more, the color drawings are then also available for any book that may be published on the making of the film, or as a special feature when the movie is released on DVD.

Storyboards come in a variety of formats. Most productions make do with black-and-white sketches that focus on camera angle and composition. The drawings are often rendered on an 8-1/2" by 11" page that is easily integrated into the script. Some directors feel that working with only one image per page gives them the freedom to manipulate individual storyboard frames into alternate sequences. Other filmmakers ask for little more than thumbnail drawings, small renditions of frames that can have up to a dozen or more stacked onto a page. The size of these frames is solely up to the director's discretion.

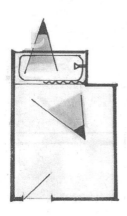

SC.173 - SHOOTING OVER BATHTUB AS THORNDYKE ENTE.

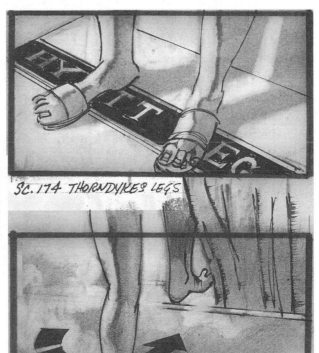

SC. 174 THORNDYKES LEGS

AS ROBE DROPS TO THE FLOOR...

[*High Anxiety*, 1977]
Director: Mel Brooks   Drawing: Harold Michelson

THE KEY FRAME

> More highly rendered than an editorial board
> Only shows highlight images from the sequence
> Often used as a sales tool
> Generally, one image per page on an 8-1/2" by 11" paper

There are times when a full editorial treatment is unwanted or unnecessary. In that case, key frames might be an appropriate substitution. Key frames pick out important moments in the story and elaborately render them, using a highly developed level of light and shadow. These frames are sometimes utilized when a producer or director is still attempting to raise money for a specific production. These drawings can act as sales tools to give the investors or studios a simple visualization of some of the proposed project's most prominent scenes. It is important to note that these drawings often fall short of being full-scale production illustrations (see below). They are meant to suggest a mood and style rather than communicate steadfast decisions. In fact, there can be a danger in showing up to a pitch meeting with too much polish on the material.

"I worked on *The Towering Inferno* as a conceptual artist and storyboarder. I boarded shots for four different camera crews. They had the stars working every day and they also had a miniature unit and a helicopter unit, and everyone had to know what everyone else was doing. The action stuff was dictated by the special effects angles chosen by the director on the miniatures. I would run back and forth between the crews and Irwin Allen, the director, says, 'Just stay ahead of me, Joe, just stay ahead.' "

— Joseph Musso
Illustrator: *The
Towering Inferno*,
Torn Curtain, *Volcano*

[*Volcano*, 1997]
Director: Mick Jackson
Drawing: Joseph Musso

PRODUCTION ILLUSTRATION

> Used to fully render lighting
> Highly detailed and polished
> Always a wide shot of the set
> Reflects the creative concepts of the Production Designer
> Used as a tool for the designer to sell set design ideas to the director and producer
> Large scale, perhaps 14" by 20" or more, one image per paper

"I also sketch most of the sets, production illustrations with quick shadows. The drawings can get expressionistic, but I try and be good, to stay with reality. I start with something quick, to get across an idea, then we focus in and I redraw and get more specific. On the major sets we also did models."

— Richard Hoover
Production designer:
Girl, Interrupted

The production illustration is a polished and highly detailed, fully realized image that depicts the setting either at a dramatic moment or without characters, as the set might be seen in an establishing shot.

There are vast sums of money devoted to the design of the settings for each production. Unless you are going to shoot at primarily existing locations, each set needs to be designed and then signed off on by the director and some combination of producers. Often, a model is built for each set. The model can either be a white version that shows only the basic structures or a fully painted maquette that features color, texture, and furnishings. Either way, the model focuses on space.

In addition to this model, many designers use production illustrations that show the set from a wide-angle view that might or might not be part of the actual shot continuity. The purpose of this drawing is twofold: One is to give a sense, in two-dimensions, of the appearance of the set. The other is to give the designer an opportunity to express his or her ideas on how the set might be lit.

[*Girl, Interrupted*, 1999]
Director: James Mangold
Drawing: Richard Hoover

COMMERCIAL STORYBOARDS (Also called Comps)

> Highly rendered color images of the commercial spot
> Reflects the creative concepts of the Advertising Agency
> Used as a sales tool to present ideas to the client
> No camera moves shown
> Standard frame up to 6″ by 8″, mounted on a board in sequence

The commercial world bears little resemblance to feature films or broadcast television as far as the use of storyboards in the initial stages of preproduction. Commercials are usually envisioned by advertising agencies, not the people who will eventually direct them. Therefore, the first storyboard is a sales tool that is commissioned by the client (e.g., a car manufacturer) and then drawn up by the agency to show their ideas on the proposed spot. Once approved, this board is then used to get directors and production companies to bid on the commercial. Once the job has been awarded, the director then has the option to create his or her own shooting boards for the spot that follow the agency's editorial storyboard structure.

[*Flying Bros*]
Drawing: John Dahlstrom

MATERIALS USED FOR THE EDITORIAL STORYBOARD

Artists use a wide variety of materials when creating an editorial story-board, ranging from a simple pencil to a state-of-the-art computer system. Most artists still employ the classic techniques of a light, rough under-sketch and then a polish level of black lines and gray-tone shadows. The materials used can include non-photo blue pencils for the under-drawing, and graphite pencils ranging from the soft, 4B variety to harder ones up to 2H for the bulk of sketching. Also, colored pencils that have a waxy content (like Prismacolor or Verithin brands) produce good, dark lines for the over-drawing details. Some artists love to add shadows with a cotton swab dipped in powdered graphite. It quickly covers large areas of the drawing, and then light can be added in by dragging an eraser over the gray-tone areas. Some artists sketch with pencil and then detail the drawing with a variety of pens and markers. These materials are less forgiving, as it is more difficult to erase or lighten up an area that has gone too dark.

Other materials that have been used in older examples of storyboards include colored pastels, gouache, watercolor, and charcoal. These materials are very beautiful in their many applications, and if you have the time, they will reward your investigations. But beware the surface — charcoal and pastel will spread and smear, so you will need to protect your originals with a fixative and/or a cover sheet.

One technique I have enjoyed starts off with sketching a simple sketch with a graphite pencil on white bond paper. I make all my overall decisions on composition and framing in this first step. Then I will make a couple of copies of the drawing onto a heavier paper and use those versions to play around with light, shadow, and maybe color, if the situation calls for it. The final version is then photocopied again and handed out to the appropriate crewmembers. This technique is time-consuming and usually used with the type of board discussed below.

MATERIALS USED IN KEY FRAME SKETCHES

Because of their use as sales tools, key frames are often rendered in color. Artists use a great variety of media for color sketches, including, but not limited to: colored pencil, pastel, watercolor, markers, pen, and charcoal. Because the key frame deals with individual setups instead of sequences, it is often rendered one to a page in the 8-1/2" by 11" format, or larger, if desired by the director or the producer.

CHOOSING YOUR MATERIALS

A description of the materials commonly used in the development of each type of board previously described is listed below. This list is meant only as a guide to your creativity. There is no single correct way to render these images. In the end, the choice of material is one that is ruled by the senses, not the intellect. Paper has a particular feel to it: smooth, rough, reflective, matte. Pencils offer a great number of qualities: hard or soft, waxy or chalky. These choices come down to personal preferences. Spend a while in an art supply store and test drive some of the materials. If you are just beginning to collect some supplies, buy a variety of pencils and see which of them responds best to your touch. Experiment. Enjoy.

The lists are by no means comprehensive, as every artist, director, or designer experiments and finds a technique that is most comfortable for her or him. This is just a general guide for those readers who may need to visit an art supply store before starting on a new project.

EDITORIAL STORYBOARDS

8-1/2″ by 11″ paper
non-photo blue pencil
graphite pencils: HB, 2B
Black pens (try Penstix, in a variety of
    widths: F, EF, EEF)
Prismacolor pencil: Black
Verithin pencil: Indigo
Sharpener
Kneaded eraser
Triangle: 90-degree with a hypotenuse
    of at least 12″

PRODUCTION ILLUSTRATIONS

Full sheets of paper 20″ by 30″ or
    illustration board
A set of gouache paints, brushes
Set of colored pencils
Graphite pencils
Toned markers
Variety of black pens

COMMERCIAL COMPS

Marker paper, 11″ by 14″
Full sets of color and gray
    tone markers
Non-photo blue pencil
Graphite pencils
Variety of black pens
Black board for mounting

KEY FRAMES

8-1/2″ by 11″ paper, or larger
    (As these can be color
    or B&W, follow the lists
    for editorial boards or
    production illustration.)

MATERIALS USED IN PRODUCTION ILLUSTRATION

Designers use a wide variety of media for this kind of sketch, including pencil, pen, pastel, charcoal, and gouache. The size of the illustrations can vary, but they are usually much larger than a typical storyboard frame — up to 20" by 30". They are typically rendered on a good sheet of illustration board or pastel paper.

MATERIALS USED IN COMMERCIAL BOARDS

Commercial boards are almost always full-color renderings. They are formatted using the television aspect ratio of 1:1.33 and are most often drawn with a set of toned markers. The boards only show composition, not camera movement. Also, the voiceover and dialogue track are inserted in a box below the image. These are highly polished images, down to the glint of light on a car's fender. They are, above all, about selling visual ideas to a client.

AN OVERVIEW

How do these four applications of preproduction visualization relate to each other?

> The **editorial board** plans out all the shots in a film to tell the story, scene by scene. The shots are then arranged in editorial sequence so that the director and the crew can refer to them during filming.

> The **key frames** only show a selection of shots, perhaps only crucial sequences or the most complex camera moves, or the establishing shot at the beginning of the scene.

> The **production illustration** isn't really a storyboard, in that it focuses on showing a set rather than a shot. It is generally created by the production designer rather than the director.

> The **commercial board** is a sales tool typically used by an advertising agency to present a concept to a client. It is often created before the director is even hired for the spot.

CASE STUDY
HIGH ANXIETY

1.

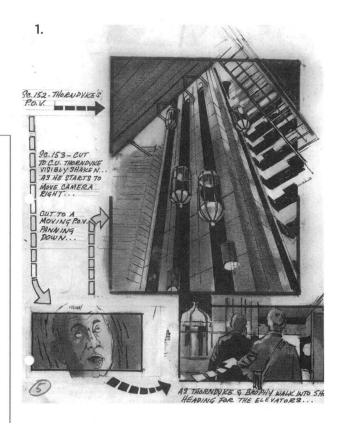

"I sat down with Hitchcock a few times when I had done a sequence that I thought was terrific. He looked at it and he said, 'This is really terrific, but I can't use it here.' And I thought, he's jealous. You know what I mean? But he was absolutely right because not only couldn't he use it, but also he explained why. A lot of people miss out because they're thinking of great shots and they lose sight of the story. And the story is a symphony that builds up to a certain thing, and this is not the place to put this absolutely sensational sequence. I was concentrating on my storyboard, which was going to be the best damn storyboard that you ever saw, except you couldn't use it there."

— Harold Michelson
Illustrator: *High Anxiety, The Birds, The Graduate*

2.

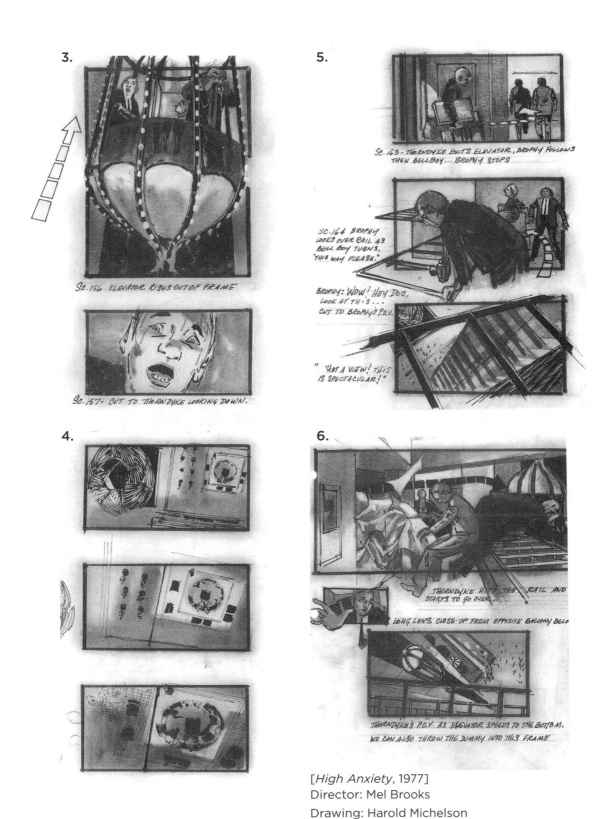

3.

Sc. 156 ELEVATOR RISES OUT OF FRAME

Sc. 157- CUT TO THORNDYKE LOOKING DOWN.

4.

5.

Sc. 163- THORNDYKE EXITS ELEVATOR, BROPHY FOLLOWS
THEN BELLBOY... BROPHY STOPS

Sc. 164 BROPHY
LOOKS OVER RAIL AS
BELL BOY TURNS,
"THIS WAY PLEASE."

BROPHY: WOW! HEY DOC,
LOOK AT THIS ...
CUT TO BROPHY'S P.O.V.

"WHAT A VIEW! THIS
IS SPECTACULAR!"

6.

THORNDYKE HITS THE RAIL AND
STARTS TO GO OVER.

LONG LENS CLOSE-UP FROM OPPOSITE BALCONY BELO

THORNDYKE'S P.O.V. AS ELEVATOR SPEEDS TO THE BOTTOM.
WE CAN ALSO THROW THE DUMMY INTO THIS FRAME

[*High Anxiety*, 1977]
Director: Mel Brooks
Drawing: Harold Michelson

"I hate the idea of going onto a location or a set someplace and [saying] 'Well, let's see, I wonder where we should put the camera?' I want to be able to say, 'The camera's going to go here, she's going to walk in the door there, and we're going to dolly with her, move in, go over there, and end up with a two-shot of her standing at the desk.' "
— Robert Wise

[*West Side Story*, 1961]
Director: Robert Wise
Production designer: Boris Levin

EDITORIAL BOARDS: THE FOCUS OF THIS BOOK

These different techniques all have their place in preproduction, but it is beyond the scope of this book to cover all of them in depth. Certainly, the skills outlined in the following chapters can be applied to any of these endeavors, but this volume will focus on the various aspects of editorial storyboarding for film and television and the relationship storyboards have to the broader process of production.

Why focus on one application? Because the editorial storyboard is the document that is most engaged with the story arc of the script. The intended audience for this information is a mixed group, made up of both filmmakers who may have limited drawing skills and artists who have a limited knowledge of film production. The editorial board, with its heavy emphasis on camera placement and character blocking, as well as the sequence of shots telling the story, gives both the director and the designer a wide margin for input and collaboration.

WHAT TO STORYBOARD? PRIORITIZING THE SCENES

When you are preparing a script for a feature film, there are situations when you have less than enough time to storyboard the entire script. You may have a modest budget that will allow you to work with a professional illustrator for only two weeks. That kind of time frame lets you visualize a few major scenes, but not much more than that. You need to prioritize the scenes to ensure that the most demanding of them will be worked out within the time and space your particular circumstance allows.

The paragraphs below cover the types of scenes that are most often storyboarded in preparation for the shoot. Some productions have the time and money to treat each scene to a thorough visualization. If you are working on a science fiction film, an action series, or a screen translation of a comic book, you may find that you have the time and budget to work on a complete visual script.

The list below is for those projects that need to concentrate their resources and storyboard a select group of scenes.

1. Special effects shots (a.k.a. FX or EFX)
2. Stunts and pyrotechnics
3. Crowd scenes
4. Action
5. Complex camera movements
6. Montage sequences
7. Opening and closing scenes

1. SPECIAL EFFECTS OR FX SHOTS are virtually always storyboarded. Most production companies do not have the internal resources to create FX shots in-house. That means that in each circumstance the work will have to be contracted out to an effects house. In order for the company to understand the production's needs, some visualization should accompany the script pages with the request for a bid on the job.

[*Cliffhanger*, 1993]
Director: Renny Harlin
Drawings: John Mann

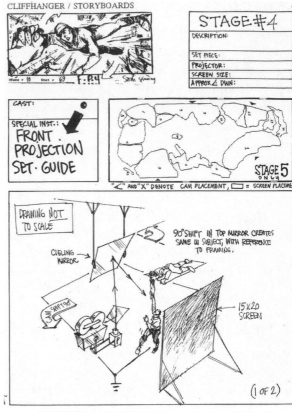

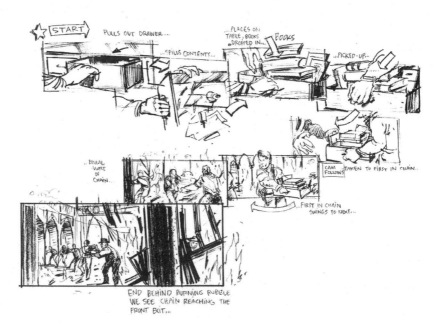

Many special effects houses have their own artists who work on visualization of the shots in question. They can work in the traditional mediums of pencil, charcoal, or marker on paper, or use advanced computer software that allows the shot to be realized in the "three dimensions" of a virtual world. Either way, the conversation between the production company, the director, and the effects group will take place as much in the visual sphere of communication as in the verbal one.

[*The Ten Commandments*, 1956]
Director: Cecil B. DeMille
Drawings: Harold Michelson

2. STUNTS AND PYROTECHNICS

are the next types of situations that will require storyboard attention. These shots are heavily choreographed and often can only be acted out one time because of cost, availability of materials, and danger to those involved. Also, multiple cameras are used in many of these cases, and the director and cinematographer will want to have as much input as possible for these second unit crews.

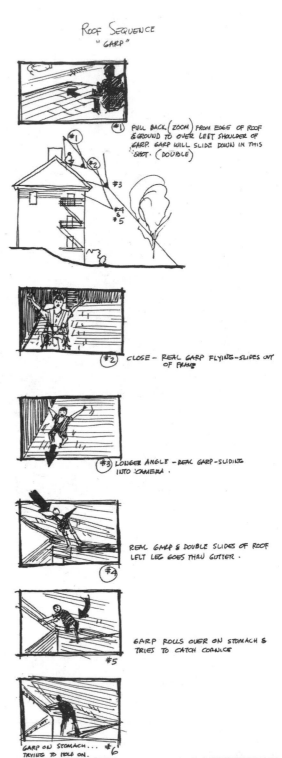

[The World According to Garp,
1982]
Director: George Roy Hill

3. CROWD SCENES are a good bet for the production that has a limited storyboarding budget. A crowd can consist of 20 or 2,000 people. At either extreme it is often useful to have a set of storyboards to hand out to a crew that may be more than taxed with the overload of bodies on the set. It is also another situation where multiple cameras may be utilized. If these sequences have already been boarded out, the director, assistant directors, and other crewmembers will have one element fewer to think about during a challenging day on the set.

[*Quo Vadis*, 1951]
Director: Mervyn LeRoy

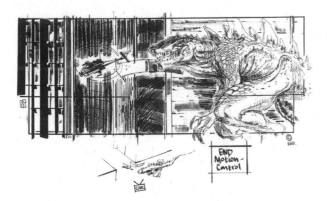

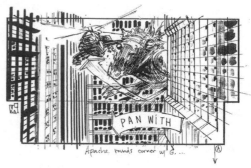

4. ACTION SEQUENCES, such as staged fights and car chases, lend themselves to storyboarding because they are usually highly choreographed, and therefore need to be visualized in great detail before the cameras roll. If an illustrator can be included in the rehearsals of the fight action, then the director will have a good visual record of the shot possibilities of that scene. Sometimes all that is necessary is a 35mm camera with a zoom or a video camera to block out the camera positions. That visual information can then be worked with to create a plan of action for photographing the action scene.

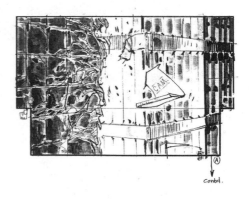

[*Godzilla*, 1998]
Director: Roland Emmerich
Drawings: John Mann

WE FOLLOW THE CHEAP SUIT INTO THE COURT ROOM... IT IS CROWDED, DISORDERLY... & MULTILINGUAL...

SC 8 ②

5. COMPLEX CAMERA MOVEMENT is another type of shot that lends itself to storyboarding. In the case of extended crane moves, handheld, or Steadicam shots, the use of overhead diagrams tied in with sketches of frame compositions can cut down rehearsal time drastically. Or they can serve as a starting point for discussions about the shot. Either way, these visual tools encourage conversation and expedite communication.

FOLLOW...
THE SEEDY MAN TAKES HIS SEAT. CAMERA PANS TO INCLUDE THE COURT OFFICER... WHO TRIES TO QUIET THE COURT ROOM
SC 8 ③ HE IS IGNORED.
QUIET.
COURT OFFICER

CAMERA MOVES PAST PEOPLE IN THE COURT ROOM TOWARD THE COURT OFFICER ...WHO...
SC 8 ④
COURT OFFICER

...AT THE SOUND OF THE JUDGE'S VOICE (THE COURT OFFICER) TURNS TOWARD THE JUDGE & MOTIVATES THE CAMERA IN THAT DIRECTION.
FIVE HUNDRED DOLLARS OR THIRTY DAYS. 3 WEEKS TO PAY!
SC 8 ⑤
COURT OFFICER

[*Nuts*, 1987]
Director: Barbra Streisand
Drawings: Carol Winstead Wood

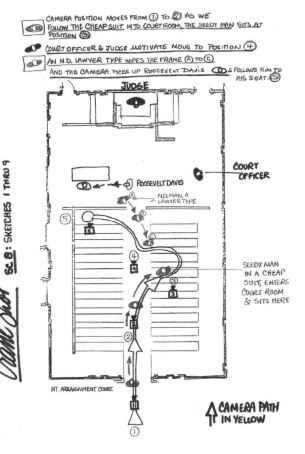

Crane Shot SC. 8: SKETCHES 1 THRU 9

CAMERA POSITION MOVES FROM ① TO ② AS WE FOLLOW THE CHEAP SUIT INTO COURT ROOM, THE SEEDY MAN SITS AT POSITION ③
COURT OFFICER & JUDGE MOTIVATE MOVE TO POSITION ④
AN N.D. LAWYER TYPE WIPES THE FRAME Ⓐ TO Ⓒ AND THE CAMERA PICKS UP ROOSEVELT DAVIS Ⓒ & FOLLOWS HIM TO HIS SEAT ⑤

JUDGE
COURT OFFICER
ROOSEVELT DAVIS
N.D. MAN, A LAWYER TYPE
SEEDY MAN IN A CHEAP SUIT, ENTERS COURT ROOM & SITS HERE
INT. ARRAIGNMENT COURT.
CAMERA PATH IN YELLOW

6. MONTAGE SEQUENCES have a specialized meaning in American filmmaking. The word "montage" was originally used by European filmmakers to mean editing in general. In the United States we have narrowed the term to apply to sequences that are edited with highly compressed time and space and usually have no dialogue. A popular example of this can be found in the shopping sequence in *Pretty Woman*, when Julia Roberts' character goes on a whirlwind tour of the best stores in Los Angeles, backed up by an instrumental rendition of the title song. An all-day expedition is related in a collage of images that edits six hours into three minutes of screen time.

Montage sequences often appear in the written script as no more than a sentence or two that instructs the director to describe a passage of time using a whirlwind of images and little or no dialogue.

The director and crew must flesh out this shot-heavy sequence visually; the storyboards, shot list, and overhead diagrams are both individually and collectively strong starting points for conversations of this type.

[*The Cotton Club*, 1984]
Director: Francis Ford Coppola
Drawings: Harold Michelson

7. OPENING AND CLOSING SE-QUENCES can also benefit from the treatment of preproduction visualization. Whether you are working on a feature-length film or a 20-minute industrial, the opening shots of a film strive to pull the audience into its particular world. The style of the film's imagery as well as the feel of its characters can be projected in those first few moments. A clear image of the shots that will make up this sequence can set the tone for the way the entire film is visualized. The same idea can apply to the closing scene of the film. If not a climactic moment, it is a denouement to the full three-act structure, and the imagery of these last moments will stay with the audience long after they leave the theater or turn off their televisions.

8. THE REST. There are no definite rights or wrongs here. This list is meant as a guide to get you started on the scenes that have the most pressing logistic need for the work. In terms of aesthetic needs, anything and everything or nothing at all can be planned in advance. The choice simply has to do with the style and the content of your individual project.

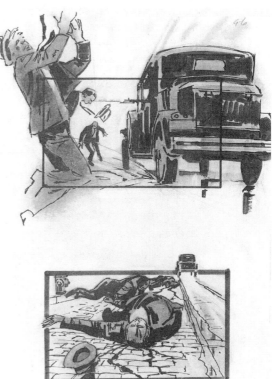

CASE STUDY
THE MILLION DOLLAR HOTEL

"The challenge of storyboarding is representing four dimensions in two. You are representing height, width, and depth on a piece of paper that only has height and width. The dimension that you have in film that you don't have in illustration is time. That is the fourth dimension. The art of storyboarding is in choosing the right moment of time for illustration. You have one frame and you must be able to take one frozen moment from that entire shot and represent it in one or two frames. You need to be able to communicate the entire shot in that one image.

"Each shot gives the audience one piece of information. The question for me as an illustrator is how I communicate that small portion of time through a single image. My background as a children's book Illustrator has helped me concentrate on this aspect of storyboarding."
— John Coven
       Illustrator: *X-Men, The Usual Suspects*

[*The Million Dollar Hotel*, 2001]
Director: Wim Wenders
Drawings: John Coven

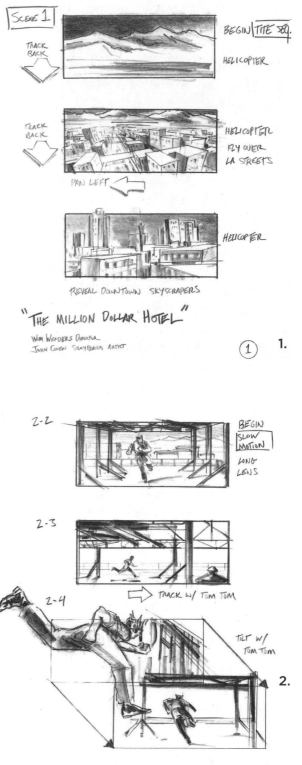

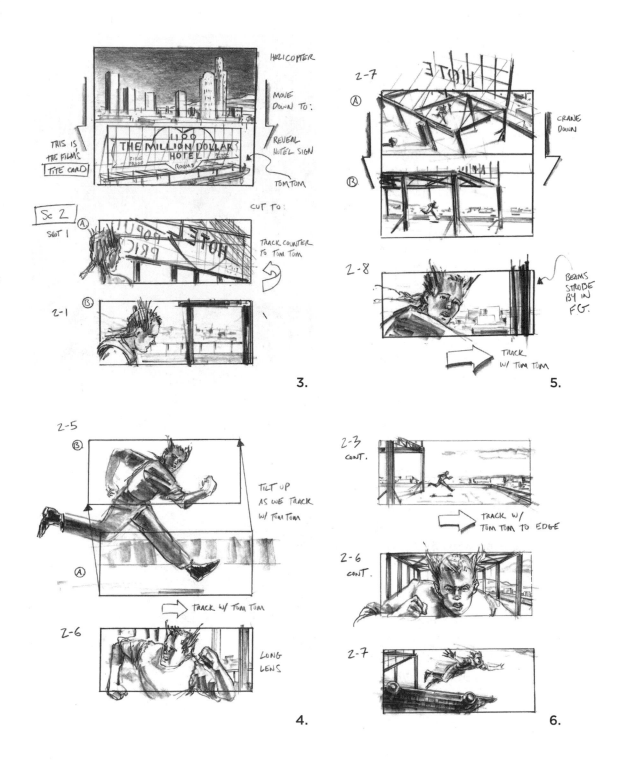

HELICOPTER

MOVE
DOWN TO:

REVEAL
HOTEL SIGN

THIS IS
THE FILM'S
TITLE CARD

1100
THE MILLION DOLLAR HOTEL
FIRE PROOF   FIRE PROOF
ROOMS

TOM TOM

CUT TO:

Sc 2
SHOT 1
A

TRACK COUNTER
TO TOM TOM

2-1   B

3.

2-7
A

CRANE
DOWN

B

2-8

BEAMS
STROBE
BY IN
F.G.

TRACK
W/ TOM TOM

5.

2-5
B

TILT UP
AS WE TRACK
W/ TOM TOM

A

TRACK W/ TOM TOM

2-6

LONG
LENS

4.

2-3
CONT.

TRACK W/
TOM TOM TO EDGE

2-6
CONT.

2-7

6.

CASE STUDY
GODZILLA

"I usually start working in pre-production about two to three months before photography. The larger sized pictures, a hundred million and up, are often very effects driven. They need to board many, many shots in order to get the picture made. So the big pictures will storyboard three-quarters or more of the film. The smaller film might only board a quarter of the movie, the action sequences and so on.

Sometimes you need to create this 'Rube Goldberg' of a story-board page. It becomes a ma-chine that you are drawing out, a dynamic operation and that takes a lot of time. On a film like *Godzilla* they expected between 10 to 20 frames a day. And that was with a high degree of polish. I've done other projects where I might whip out up to sixty draw-ings in a single day and night. But I told the director that they were not going to be pretty drawings."

— John Mann
Illustrator: *Godzilla*

THE STORYBOARDING MEETING: WHO IS INVOLVED?

How many artists does it take to concoct a board? The answer is as individual as each director's taste. Some directors, such as Martin Scorsese and Werner Fassbinder, prefer to work on their own, sketching small images to be used as personal notes during production. Others draw up rough sketches themselves and then hand the drawings over to a skilled illustrator to polish them up before distributing them to the crew. George Roy Hill worked in this way on *The World According to Garp* and *The Great Waldo Pepper*.

Still others like to use their designers or illustrators as visual assistants and work out the shot list and camera positions with them. Then, artists take these notes and translate them into storyboards based on these conversations. And some directors will hand over scenes without much input at all and allow the collaborator to visualize the sequence. Once the storyboard is finished, the director will edit the images and perhaps ask for revisions.

"…we go through everything scene by scene. I'm really meticulous about this. It's a part of choices that you make in terms of composition, lighting, and staging. What I like to do is talk about the big picture. I write these incredibly long memos about the full vision of the film. It gives the visual department a step-by-step idea of where the character starts, what's the point of view, how that point of view evolves, and what the conclusion is in the end. When a prop guy asks, 'What kind of drinking glass should I get — one with Miss Piggy on it, or should I get the Pyrex kind?' he has been let in on the bigger picture of the film so that we can make the choice in a way that is more realistic."
— Jodi Foster
    Director: *Little Man Tate, Home for the Holidays*

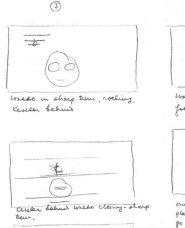

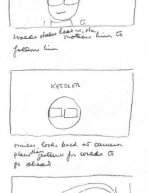

[*The Great Waldo Pepper*, 1975]
Director: George Roy Hill
Drawings: George Roy Hill

I have worked with directors at both ends of the "input spectrum," from those who stood over my shoulder expressly manipulating the angle and composition of each shot to those who handed over a script and told me to come back in a few days with a few scenes boarded out. The majority fall somewhere between the extremes, feeling comfortable with giving suggestions, but not feeling that they had to control the entire enterprise.

If I were given a choice, I would like a director to bring an overhead diagram to our storyboard meeting. The diagram includes both abstract and concrete information and is extremely useful to someone trying to visualize the composition of each shot on the

[*Key Largo*, 1948]
Director: John Huston

list. Some directors will bring in an overhead diagram with actors' movements already worked out. Sometimes there is the time, money, and inclination to rehearse extensively before principal photography. Other times the storyboarding process itself is the extent of the preproduction work on some scenes.

If a director comes to a meeting with one of the three visualization documents already developed, the visual assistant will then help to expand that work into a more complete document for the crew. I have gotten up with directors and acted out the scenes with them as we blocked the characters. I have had discussions about motivation of camera moves and the logistics of moving around small locations. The storyboard artist needs to be knowledgeable in editing and composition as well as illustration. The needs of the director vary enormously from project to project, and only by being fluent in the many facets of filmmaking will a visual assistant be able to effectively communicate in the necessary language of the moment.

WHEN AND WHERE TO BEGIN THE STORYBOARD PROCESS

The attitude toward this aspect of the process varies from director to director. Some find that drawing and diagramming very early in the process helps them to begin solidifying their ideas about the film. Others prefer to wait until the locations have been locked down and the sets designed before they begin this type of planning.

VISUALIZATION TIMELINE CHART

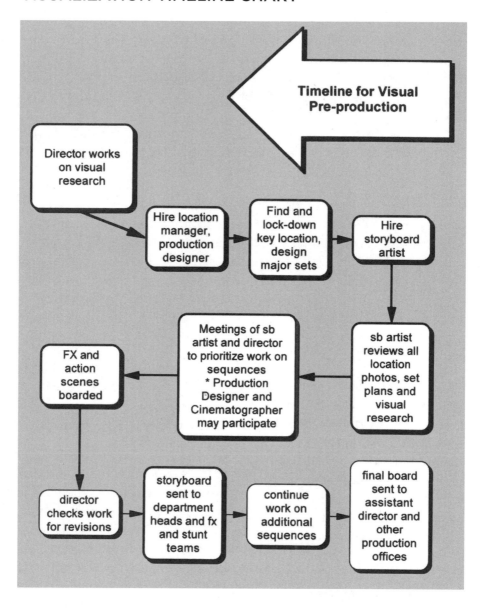

USE OF RESEARCH MATERIALS

When working in collaboration it is important for a director to share his or her visual sources with whoever is brought into the process. Clips from films, magazine pages, and books on art and photography all aid in the communication of a general style or individual shots. If there is time, watch films together and discuss the influence of different sequences, camera angles, and lighting schemes in terms of the project at hand. Often this topic is only discussed between the cinematographer and the director, but opening up the discussion to include the illustrator and the other visual collaborators can allow the crew to be more aligned with the director's vision.

Once the style is developed and understood by all involved, the director can sit down alone or with a partner and begin to clarify ideas in specific images, shot lists, and overhead diagrams. Some people choose to work from images into words, others start with the shot list, then look at an overhead of the set and then place the camera in the positions it needs to occupy in order to cover the action. Other directors start with the overhead diagram, block out the actors' movements first, and then place the camera in position to watch the scene play out.

"I can't not draw stuff and I can't not say it should be done this way. But it's a collaborative thing. I have very specific ideas and either I draw them or I drag in references and say 'I want you to look at this.' But, if you get good people, they can interpret this and make it work.... I like working with good people because if I come up with an idea, they come up with a better idea, then I come up with an even better one, and so on: it's a leap-frog process, and the work becomes much better than it would be if only I did exactly what I want."

— Terry Gilliam
Gilliam on Gilliam, 1999

LOCATIONS AND SETS: TIMING STORYBOARD PROCESS TO REAL SPACE

There are times when the production schedule is so rushed that the process of preparing the visual documents is left to the last two weeks or even the last few days of preproduction. This scenario is not terrific for anyone involved. The director is usually overwhelmed by other demands of the production. Location scouting for new sets, actor rehearsals, meetings with the cinematographer, even last-minute casting decisions demand the director's time. This means that end-run decision making is often done by the supporting staff (i.e., the assistant) and then looked over and approved or changed by the director on the fly.

[*Monty Python
and the Holy Grail*, 1974]
Director: Terry Gilliam
Director's drawing

Now, some people work best under pressure, but my suggestion is that if you have some of the locations identified and a few sets designed early in the process (say, one to two months before shooting), then waste no time and get to the task. Aesthetic decisions made in a calm state of mind are likely to be more true to your artistic sensibility than those made in the heat of pressure. And even if this isn't true for your style of creativity, you can always change your mind about the storyboard as you get closer to the shooting day. It is good to know that you have at least one draft of the visual script available.

DISSOLVE TO-

[*Ben-Hur*, 1959]
Altered location photographs
Director: William Wyler
Art director: Ed Carfagno

WORKING ON LOCATION

> Tools: digital still or video camera
> Floor plans drawn to scale and reduced for easy in-script use
> Sketch artist to create visual record of rehearsals

[*Destination Tokyo*, 1943]
Director: Delmer Daves

CASE STUDY
SISTER, SISTER

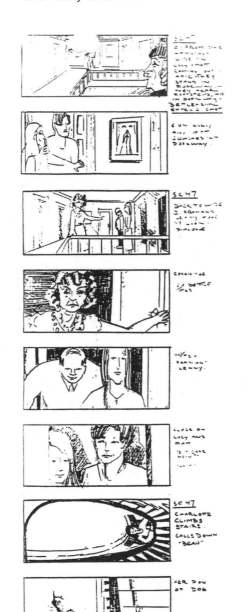

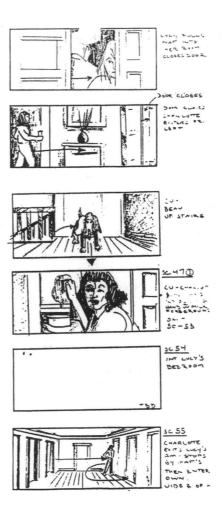

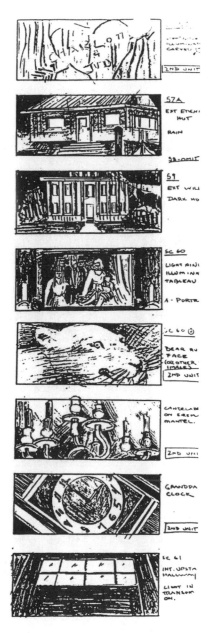

[*Sister, Sister*, 1987]
Director: Bill Condon
Drawings: Marcie Begleiter

In 1985 I worked with a writer who was preparing to shoot his first feature as director. The producer on this film was an experienced hand who realized that the more input the young director received in terms of story visualization, the better off the production would be when it came to shooting and editing the footage. I was hired on two months before principal photography was to begin. We spent the first week in a screening room viewing films that had influenced the director regarding the style of the project. The script was of the gothic-suspense genre and took place in the sweltering backwoods of Louisiana.

We immersed ourselves in the work of Hitchcock, Robert Aldrich, and Fritz Lang, not to mention books on photography and painting that related to the setting and period of the story. I began to draw the first scene: a lyrical, dreamlike montage of images. The director and producer approved these first efforts and within two weeks we were on our way down to Louisiana to finish the bulk of preproduction on location.

There were four of us in the team; the director, the cinematographer, the production designer, and myself, the storyboard artist. We walked through every location and talked through the scenes shot by shot. I kept notes, took photographs, and participated in the discussions that ranged from general ideas about the color scheme to specific decisions regarding the placement of the camera. By the end of three weeks we had completed the essential scene work, and I continued to draw up the storyboard images that were the visual notes of these meetings. By the time the crew arrived and started preparing for the shoot, we had the majority of the script worked out in a shot list and storyboard frames.

The producer and the director then made an unusual and very interesting request. I was asked to take the storyboards and reduce all the images on an office Xerox machine so that they could be handed out in a condensed form. I had been working on the scenes in editorial order, but the production wanted to hand out copies of the boards to the heads of all the crews, and requested the images in shooting order, with the shots for a day's work on a single sheet.

This handout elicited unexpected comments from my coworkers. The sound technician thanked me for the information. He said it let him plan ahead for what would be required. "Now I've got an idea of which boom to carry into the swamp tonight," he said with grateful amusement. It was a hard shoot, with lots of night work and a fairly unforgiving schedule. I was around for the first two weeks of shooting — one of the characters in the film was a painter and I had been hired to create a series of canvases for her character — and was delighted to see the director walk onto the set each day with the storyboard sheet sticking out of his back pocket.

> "I never make storyboards, designs. In fact, I write out my own scenes and then, in the moment of shooting, I really do the opposite of what I have written, generally speaking."
>
> — **Bernardo Bertolucci**
> *Directing the Film*

Months later when I went to see the completed film at the cast and crew screening, I was amazed to find that watching the movie was like seeing the storyboard come to life. There was approximately an 80-90% correlation between the boards and the film as it was shot and edited. To this day I feel that this was one of the high points in my experiences as a film collaborator. And I credit the experience to the producer, who had the foresight to spend a little extra up-front so that the work of visualizing the film was a priority. The storyboard in that production was a document that came out of a true collaboration of the director, designers, cinematographer, and illustrator.

FROM THE GENERAL TO THE SPECIFIC

The information in this chapter has been intended as a general guide to the process of preproduction visualization. The chapters that follow will cover the specifics of creating the storyboard, the shot list, and the overhead diagram. The information needed to create them will be explained in detail and exercises will be offered to focus and develop your visual communication skills.

POINTS TO REMEMBER:

> Prioritize your scenes
> Decide on the crew members to be involved with the pre-viz
> Start well ahead of shooting schedule
> Work off of location overheads and floor plans of the set whenever possible
> Determine who will receive the boards and distribute

[*The Ten Commandments*, 1956]
Director: Cecil B. DeMille
Drawings: Harold Michelson

VISUAL EFFECTS ART DIRECTOR AT DIGITAL DOMAIN

"At Digital Domain [an EFX house in Los Angeles], I primarily develop ideas on the computer in 3D programs like Bryce 4, Photoshop, and Poser. I also create animatics and make quick-time movies to illustrate the shots for those directors who need help visualizing what they want. So the more complete storyboard you can provide for them the better. I'll take drawings and flesh them out in 2D and 3D software. These are my equivalents of storyboards, but they're basically key frame illustrations. They will carry you through a live-action sequence.

At Digital Domain we are often approached by directors who bring us a script and ask us to identify which elements need digital effects, or sometimes they come to us with key frames and ask us to flesh them out. It depends on how active the production designer and the director are together on planning the digital effects. Many directors lack experience in that area and they leave it to the visual effects supervisor. The job is relatively new; it's just been used for the last few years, and the visual effects art director is even newer. I acquired that title for myself a few years ago when I was brought onto *The Fifth Element*.

On a picture like that there might be five key people working on a single sequence: one working on the camera move, someone else working on the models, another working on the lighting, and another on the 2D and 3D elements. Then we have a leader who oversees everyone and acts as an administrator. The hierarchy might look like this: the Visual Effects Supervisor over the Digital Effects Supervisor and then the Art Directors reporting to them, just like any other film crew. Then there is — on top of all that — the executive producer, who has the final say.

Sometimes the director might like to talk to me rather than filter the information through someone else. Once I've done the still frames or an animatic I'll take it to the Visual Effects Supervisor, who will give me feedback, and then the material goes to the artists again, version through version. Sometimes there might be 50 or 60 iterations of a visual effect before it finally gets approved by the director in the screening room."

THE FIFTH ELEMENT
EFFECTS DRAWINGS BY RON GRESS

> **preliminary drawing**

> **3D digital storyboard**

> **film frame**

[*The Fifth Element*, 1997]
Director: Luc Besson
Drawings: Ron Gress

IT'S TWO IN THE MORNING...

I was working as a set decorator on a non-union feature. It was Friday, and since there was no turnaround time minimum for the actors, we were all being worked far into the night. We were working at a bar location and had been on the set for close to fourteen hours. The second meal of the evening had been lukewarm pizza, and nerves were fraying. The director sat at the bar between shots, staring at his script and trying to come up with the next setup of the evening. There wasn't a shot list or storyboard in sight. The director stared. He mumbled. He conferred. We were all tired, hungry, and ready to pull a mutiny. Finally, the key grip couldn't take it anymore. He strode over to the director and laid out the sequence for him. Loudly, with hand gestures. The crew exchanged quiet glances. "Good idea, let's shoot it," said the director.

Inspiration can come from any direction, in any form. But a storyboard and/or a shot list would have shown the crew that the director had done his homework. At two in the morning, any leadership is appreciated.

Sketch: Sergei Eisenstein

THREE APPROACHES TO COMMUNICATION

Many years ago I had lost my keys at a friend's house and stood in his hallway with my eyes closed, silently trying to remember where I had put them. He watched me for a while and then said with astonishment, "You're looking for the keys in your head, aren't you? You're playing back a movie of where you've been in the house and watching the images with your mind's eye." I was puzzled. "Of course," I said. "How do you find things?" "I make a list," he replied. I was stunned. Making lists to find objects was inconceivable to me.

> "It is exactly what we do in cinema, combining shots that are depictive, single in meaning, neutral in content — into intellectual contexts and series."
>
> —Sergei Eisenstein "Cinematographic Principle and the Ideogram," *Film Form*, 1929

Then I had one of those "aha" moments: I realized I had made assumptions about the way other people process the world around them.

Some people understand the world primarily through words, others through images. If we examine the differences between these two approaches, we can uncover valuable information that can be used in strategizing communication within a film crew or any other collaborative project.

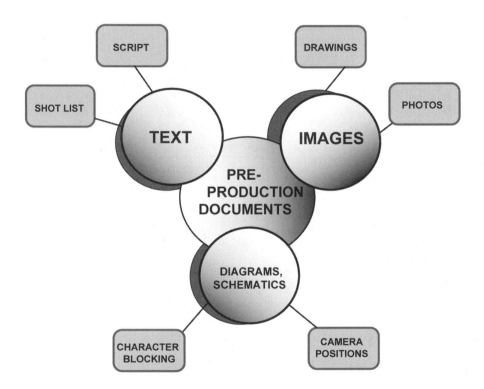

The human mind is a complex, multitasking "machine" that is capable of many varieties of thought and expression. The left hemisphere is considered to control logic and language formation, while the right hemisphere is credited with creative and intuitive functions. When constructing the storyboard document, we want to acknowledge this variation in thinking and include information that works on multiple levels.

Using a combination of text, images, and diagrams acknowledges that people react to these different forms of communication in varying degrees. While some of your collaborators will cull useful information from the overhead diagram, others will head straight to the images.

With this process in mind, this chapter is divided into sections detailing these three types of preproduction documents: the Shot List, the Overhead Diagram, and the Images that accompany and illustrate them.

TEXT	*SCRIPT, SHOT LIST*
DIAGRAM	*OVERHEAD, SCHEMATIC PLOT PLAN, FLOOR PLAN*
IMAGE	*DRAWING* *PHOTO* *CGI (COMPUTER GENERATED IMAGERY)*

PRODUCTION NAME: rko # 522   No. P.10333

SC. # 35: INT. BAR, NIGHT _____ DATE SHOT **Monday** **30 Sept:**

SLATES PRINTED	TIME FIRST SETUP GIVEN	TIME CAMERA READY	TIME FIRST TAKE	TIME SCENE COMPLETED	DESCRIPTION OF ANGLES, ACTION AND DIALOGUE
1X-3 50'	7.30	7.45	8.15	8.25 .15	Shot 1: C/U of the bar top with glasses in F.G.
2X-1 60'	8.35	8.55	8.57	8.58 .13	TRACK with bartender as he fills glasses. Med. shot with bar in mirror refection
3X-3 50'	9 (Waiting for	9.30	10.40 Bill	10.50 .27	Cut to door of bar, full shot, frontal angle. Door opens slowly letting in the light.
4X-1 30'	11 ('Waiting for	11.5	11.15	11.16 .9	Med. shot of Jake scanning the crowd.
5X-2 25'	11.20	11.30	11.35	11.40	POV, PANNING the bar right and left, wide shot.
6X-6 20' T.2.Fair.T.4.Look	11.58	12 short.T.5.	12.3 slow.Flicke	12.5 .10	Reaction shots of the bar patrons, various angles
7X-1 30' Lunch 1.230 - 1.	1	1.15	1.20	1.25 .9	ECU of Jakes feet as he walks down the bar. TRACK back to follow.

[Shot list from *Vertigo*, 1958]
Director: Alfred Hitchcock

> "I aim to get a complete vision of my film before it goes onto the studio floor. With a first-class director the final cutting is a simple job, if he has constructed the scene in his mind in advance and knows what he wants to create."
> — Alfred Hitchcock
> *Hitchcock on Hitchcock*

THE TEXT:
SHOT LISTS AND TERMINOLOGY

The "text" in this chapter refers to the words of the shot list. The shot list is a written collection of shot descriptions, each containing information on the placement of the camera and the contents of the frame. In order to accurately convey this information, the shot list needs to use precise language that delineates the action of the scene as well as the position of the camera and its movements.

A visually specific shot list needs to include the following information:

> Scale
> Angle
> Camera movement
> Blocking (of characters, vehicles, etc.)
> Script notations

SCALE: The relationship of the frame to the objects it presents. The frame crops the world into rectangular-shaped vistas. If the frame crops a human figure just below the shoulders, you have a close-up. If the frame allows the viewer to see an entire village, you've got a wide shot.

ANGLE: The relationship of the camera's position to the object(s) it is focusing on. The angle describes the position of the camera in terms of height as well as horizontal placement. If the camera is below a window and straight on, the angle is low and frontal. If the camera is facing someone's head and is located a bit to the side, it is a three-quarter close-up, eye level.

CAMERA MOVEMENT: This term refers to the movement of the camera during a shot. It can be as subtle as a slight tilt to keep a character centered in the frame or a swooping crane shot that covers dozens of feet in a few seconds. Each camera move also has a screen direction — the right and left of the camera as seen by someone looking through the lens. The screen direction is the opposite of stage direction: If an actor were to cross to stage left (the actor's left) on a line of dialogue, then the camera would need to move screen right to follow.

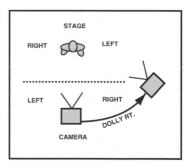

CHARACTER BLOCKING: Although the shot list primarily gives information on camera placement and movement, there can also be references to the movement of what is being seen inside the frame. This includes actors' entrances and exits from the frame, movement of vehicles, or any other action that could affect the continuity of the sequence.

```
                          stripes.  Don't you go and get any ideas.
                          Got it?

                      His father shakes his head in frustration.  Then, as before,
                      the kitchen is quiet, everyone in their own thoughts.

SHOT 16        EXT. SMALL HOUSE - DAY - FLASHBACK                    #17· 4/0/34
Insert -       A shovel is thrust into the hard thick dirt.  Robbie, sweaty
  high         and dirty, digs a hole for his father.  His mother steps out     #18-
               from the house carrying a glass of water.                         full big -
                                                                                 format
                                   MOTHER
                              Here you go, honey.         Cut back - 17
                      Robbie takes the glass, wipes the sweat from his brow.  After
                      taking a sip he hands the glass back to his mother who stands
                      for a moment watching Robbie resume shoveling.         insert ?

           #19                  MOTHER
          Med-Lw4        Sometimes I wish we lived in one of those
                              suburb neighborhoods.  Course then we'd
                              be just like everyone else.  Have the
                              same house, same car, same job. . . same      use
                              paycheck.                                       as
                                                                            master
                      She thinks for a second.

                                   MOTHER
                              Maybe being different like we are isn't
                              so bad. . . What do you think?
```

From student project:
  Damon O'Steen

SCRIPT NOTATIONS: In order to keep the storyboard tightly aligned with the script, small sections of dialogue or descriptions of action are sometimes added to the shot list or included in storyboard subtitles. These notations are direct quotes from the script and identify the placement of shots in relation to the action of the screenplay. For instance, a set of storyboard frames describing some over-the-shoulder shots might be accompanied by snippets of dialogue from the script marking the length of each shot.

SHOT LIST TERMINOLOGY

There is a saying that "a picture is worth a thousand words." But in a shot list you don't have that much space. Familiarity with the language of filmmaking is essential to creating concise descriptions of each shot. In the pages that follow, terms that apply to the **SCALE**, **ANGLE**, **CAMERA MOVEMENT**, and **CHARACTER BLOCKING** are defined in words, diagrams, and images. This section is an illustrated glossary of film language that can be used to create a precise shot list.

SCALE

EXTREME CLOSE-UP (E.C.U.): A shot with a very narrow field of view that gives the impression that the camera is very close to the subject. For instance, a part of a person's face.

CLOSE-UP (C.U.): Same as above, but with a slightly larger field of view. A character's head and shoulders, for example.

MEDIUM SHOT (M.S.): A shot in which the field of view is between those of the long shot and the close-up. The camera sees the actor from the waist up.

AMERICAN SHOT (also called Hollywood, Cowboy, or Knee shot): A shot that frames a figure from the knees up.

FULL FIGURE: Shot composed around the scale of a full human figure.

LONG SHOT (L.S.): A shot giving a broad view of the visual field; the camera appears to be far away from the subject (the z axis).

WIDE SHOT (W.S.): Shot composed to see a wide vista (the x axis).

SINGLE: A shot with only one person.

TWO SHOT: The camera frames two characters in a scene.

INSERT: Often photographed by the second unit, this shot, frequently a close-up, reveals details not seen in the master shot or missed by the general coverage, e.g., a hand opening a purse and pulling out a gun.

TWO-T SHOT: Not exactly a politically correct term; it means a shot framed from the nipples up.

ANGLE

HIGH ANGLE: A shot taken from an angle above the object.

AERIAL SHOT: A very high angle shot, often accomplished with a helicopter or an airplane.

LOW ANGLE: A shot taken from the placement of the camera below the object.

HIGH HAT SHOT: A very low angle shot, positioned as if it were a hat's height off the floor. The name is taken from a piece of equipment called a high hat, which is laid on the floor and is designed to hold the camera.

3/4 SHOT: A shot that is positioned halfway between a frontal angle and a profile. Can be either a front or a back shot.

PROFILE: Shot from a side angle.

STRAIGHT ON, OR FRONTAL: When the camera is looking directly at an object.

OVER THE SHOULDER SHOT (O.T.S.): Usually a shot of a character in conversation with a second person, whose shoulder you shoot over.

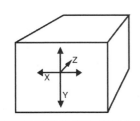

CANTED FRAME: Also called a "dutch" angle. The camera is tilted sideways, setting the objects off the vertical axis.

3 DIMENSIONS OF MOVEMENT

CAMERA MOVES

DOLLY TO FOLLOW

DOLLY SHOT: Also called "tracking" or "trucking" shot. Camera travels on dolly tracks. Usually used to describe shots moving on the z axis (pushing in or pulling out).

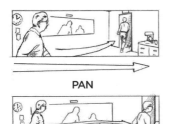

PAN

TRACK

PAN: The camera swivels on the horizontal (x) axis, often used to follow the action.

SWISH PAN: A very swift pan that blurs the scene in between the starting and ending points.

TRACKING SHOT: Camera moves to left or right. Often used to follow a figure or vehicle.

TILT: The camera pivots up and down from its base, which does not move.

BOOM SHOT: The camera travels up and down on a boom arm. Often combines with a dolly move.

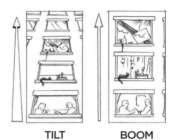

TILT   BOOM

CRANE SHOT: A shot taken from a crane that has the ability to boom down and track in long distances without using tracks.

CAR MOUNT: A shot taken from a camera that is mounted directly onto a vehicle.

STATIC SHOT: Any shot where the camera specifically does not move.

CAR MOUNT

STEADICAM SHOT: A shot using the Steadicam, a camera that attaches to a harness and can be operated by a single person in handheld situations; the resulting footage will appear to be shot with the smoothness of a tracking shot.

ZOOM: Refers to the movement of a zoom lens. Usually used in video.

ZOOM

ZOLLY: A technique in which the camera dollies in and zooms out at same time, or the reverse-zoom in and dolly out simultaneously. Also called a Dolly with counter zoom. See Hitchcock (*Vertigo*), Spielberg (*Jaws*), Scorsese (*Goodfellas*).

SMASH ZOOM: Very fast zoom.

HANDHELD: Operator braces the camera on the shoulder or at hip height. Often used in point-of-view shots or in documentary-style footage.

FOLLOW SHOT: Any moving shot that follows an actor.

TRAVELING SHOT: Any shot that utilizes a moving camera body (a dolly is a traveling shot, a pan isn't).

EDITING, TRANSITIONS, AND CAMERA POINT OF VIEW

> "To envision information, and what bright and splendid visions can result, is to work at the intersection of image, word, number, art."
>
> — Edward Tufte
> *Envisioning*
> *Information*

OBJECTIVE SHOT: The camera sees the scene from an angle not seen by a character in the scene.

SUBJECTIVE SHOT: A shot taken from the position of someone in the scene. A Point of View (P.O.V.) shot is an example of a subjective shot.

MASTER SHOT: Also called a Cover shot. Usually a medium to wide-angle shot of a scene that runs for the duration of the action.

ESTABLISHING SHOT: Often a wide shot of the location. It tells the audience where they are.

COVERAGE: All the setups needed to edit the scene aside from the master shot.

SETUP: Refers to the position of a camera and the lighting of a shot or shots. A "new setup" means that the camera is moving to a new position, which also requires re-lighting.

OFF SCREEN (O.S.): Also called O.C., off-camera. A description of what is heard but not seen on the screen.

REACTION SHOT: Usually a close-up of a character reacting silently to action they have just seen or dialogue they are listening to.

REACTION SHOT

CUTAWAY: An editing term concerning a piece of information not seen in the master or previous shot.

JUMP CUT: Editing term for successive shots that cut in on the same axis. Also, successive cuts that disrupt the flow of time or space.

IN-LINE EDIT: Contemporary term for cutting on the same axis.

MATCH CUT, OR MATCH DISSOLVE: Cutting or dissolving from one similar composition to another, e.g., from a close-up of a wheel to a shot of a globe of the world, so that both objects fill the same size and position in the frame.

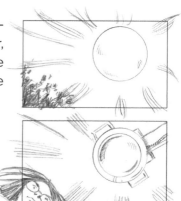

POINT OF VIEW SHOT (P.O.V.): The camera takes the point of view of a character in the scene; it sees what the character sees. Usually follows a shot of the character.

REVERSE SHOTS

REVERSE ANGLE: A shot that is 180 degrees opposite of the preceding shot.

EXERCISE: BACKWARDS SHOT LIST
Creating a Visually Precise Shot List

When studying an art, whether it be painting, music, or filmmaking, copying "the masters" can be an illuminating and instructive exercise. As you copy a Rembrandt drawing, you are compelled to look very carefully at each decision he made regarding the composition, light, and shadow of the work. In film-making you can achieve a similar study by working back from the completed film to recreate a preproduction document.

I call this project the "Backwards Shot List," because you take a sequence that has already been shot and edited and create a shot list, working in the opposite of the normal progression.

1. Choose a film that you want to study. It can be one that you've already seen or one that you've always wanted to get to know.

2. Play the film on DVD. Try to obtain a letterboxed copy so you will see the frame as it was meant to be seen. Make sure that you can see a clear image on your screen when you pause the film.

3. Watch the entire film and make some general notes on scenes or sequences that you find compelling.

4. You will need a sequence that has 20 to 30 shots in it. That means separate shots, not counting cutbacks to setups that have been previously used.

5. Play the scene you've selected, pausing the film at each cut or other transition. Write down a description of each shot, making sure that you describe the scale, angle, camera movement, and character blocking. (See examples 1 and 2, below.)

[*Paths of Glory*, 1957]

Ex. 1 Low angle two shot of soldier and guard. Soldier is C.U. in foreground, guard med. frame left.

Ex. 2 Start shot on a full, 3/4 angle of soldier as he stands and begins to cross camera right. PAN right to follow and TRACK slightly to clear attorney's back. End shot on a profile, full figure of soldier facing judges.

6. Number the shots, referring to cut-backs by the number that they were first assigned.

7. Shots that use a moving camera will need to be described twice: once to describe how they appear at the start and a second time for the end of the shot. In addition, describe how the camera has moved to get from the opening position to the ending one.

You will find that this exercise will sharpen your eyes to better understand the filmmaker's decisions regarding composition and camera angle, as well as editing. And for those of you who are new to the vocabulary of filmmaking, it will give you an opportunity to become familiar with the language.

5 ELEMENTS OF A VISUAL SHOT LIST

1. Scale

2. Angle

3. Camera Move

4. Character Blocking

5. Dialogue or Action

OVERHEAD DIAGRAMS

Overhead diagrams are the most powerful, universally communicative documents you can offer to your collaborators. They can sketch out the placement of the camera for different setups, the blocking of the actors in relation to their environment, and the position of key set pieces.

The overheads are also referred to as plot plans, floor plans, or schematics. Often the production designer or art director will sketch out each location and set design to scale. Reductions of these large drawings are perfect to use as a basis for planning out camera positions and scene blocking.

Key to understanding these documents is a familiarity with the "visual shorthand" of design. Through the use of well-placed icons, color, line width, and other eye-grabbing devices, you can lead the viewer's attention to crucial information. The following section covers some of the usual strategies for getting the point across.

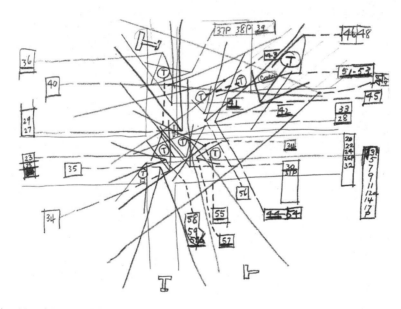

[*North by Northwest*, 1958]
Overhead diagram of the crop
duster sequence

CAMERA POSITION AND NUMBERING

Each overhead diagram sets out to plot the blocking of the characters and the positions of the camera or cameras for a scene or sequence of shots. The shots are often listed in an editorial sequence and numbered accordingly. The shot list that may accompany the diagram will also be numbered, and these two documents should agree in their sequencing so that the numbers of the shot list match the numbers that mark the camera positions.

In cases where multiple cameras are being used, each camera needs its own label. You can use letters, numerals, or crew designations, anything that will get across the idea that you are assigning positions to distinctly separate camera crews.

There are times that the information needed on a particular scene or sequence is just too voluminous for a single diagram. In this case, make copies of the floor plan and plot out a portion of the information on one sheet and the rest on a second one. Layering sheets of translucent paper is another solution to the problem of tightly packed information. Using a bottom layer of white paper, start with a floor plan and then layer each scene's blocking and camera positions on subsequent layers. For reproduction, just use a single overlay and copy with the original floor plan as a back-up sheet.

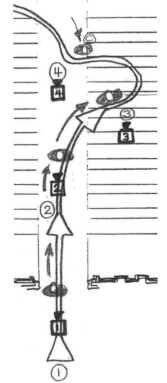

Moving cameras offer another challenge. The camera has a starting point, an ending point, and a path in between. The multiple positions are still part of a single camera move, so the corresponding shot list number will be the same. To keep things clear, subnumbering the different positions of the move is a good idea. A Steadicam shot might have four important key frames to hit on its way to its final position. Each of these should be noted on the diagram and, if an illustrated storyboard is being created, then these key positions should also be treated in corresponding frames.

[*Nuts*, 1979]
Overhead diagram (detail)

ARROWS

Big and little, straight and curved, with or without drop-shadows, these symbols denote direction of movement — actors walking, cars riding, or cameras rolling down the road. Arrows are one of the most powerful visual tools that you can use in overhead diagrams. They quickly attract the eye and can be used to guide the reader through the document. In addition, they can be designed to be visually distinct from each other, using dashes, line weight, or other clues to distinguish one character's blocking from another.

COLOR/VALUE

Imagine a vast plane of black and white squares and then, over to the right side, a red dot intrudes on the scene. Where does your eye go? When used strategically, color can attract the eye. When you want to emphasize an element of information or separate it from the rest, then using color can be key.

Although many offices have ready access to color reproduction, the cost is often far higher than it is for black-and-white copies. For this reason, it is advisable to print pre-viz images in both formats to assure that all the visual information is communicated clearly, with and without color cues.

LINE WEIGHT AND DESIGN

Thick or thin, dashes or dots, wavy or straight — even in a black-and-white document you can communicate a variety of information through simple variations of line weight and the size and shape of your lines and arrows. You can give each character a different line weight or style; you can use thick lines for camera moves and thin for character blocking. There is no industry standard for these choices. Just select a style that works for you and be consistent.

ICONS

An icon is a simple representation of an object or idea. A red sign with a picture of a hand held out is an icon for the idea of "stop." In diagramming for film, video, or other media, icons can stand in for the camera, actors, or other objects about which information needs to be communicated to the crew.

The camera icon can be expressed in a number of simple forms. A small box with an angled "v" attached gives the position and a direction for the lens. Some directors do away with the box and simply draw two extended lines to show the camera's orientation. Whatever form appeals to you, use it. Just remember to keep it simple.

Tracks, pans, Steadicam shots, and other camera moves have their own icons for use in the overhead. Please refer to the diagrams on this page and the next for some additional ideas regarding these and other objects often found in an overhead.

CREATE A LEGEND

A legend is the key to a diagram's overall interpretation. If you use icons to represent your camera, characters, or their movements, a legend is a helpful guide for the reader to decipher your meaning. The legend can be placed in a corner of the diagram or along the top edge. Just don't let it interfere with the main portion of the information. Since each director, cinematographer, or designer may use his or her own icons for the camera or actors, the legend offers a quick method of identification.

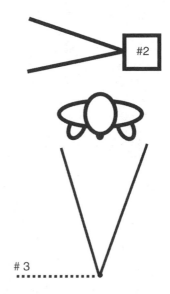

CAMERA AND FIGURE ICONS FOR OVERHEAD DIAGRAMS

EXERCISE: OVERHEAD DIAGRAMMING

This project will familiarize you with using icons to map out the positioning of cameras and characters in a scene from a film that has already been shot and edited.

1. Choose a film that you would like to study and know more intimately. You might consider a film directed by Orson Welles, Stanley Kubrick, Alfred Hitchcock, or Jane Campion.

2. Choose a scene from the film that has at least 10 shots. As you watch the scene again, attempt to create a proportional overhead of the environment with all the major walls, doors, furniture, streets, and buildings in place relative to each other.

3. Once this is done, watch the scene a third time, pausing on each shot. Then, on the diagram, place a camera icon in the appropriate position for each of the shots. If the camera moves during the shot, be sure to indicate both the starting and the ending positions.

EXERCISE EXAMPLE:
PATHS OF GLORY,
THE COURTROOM SEQUENCE

In the following example, the overhead diagram is accompanied by still frames from *Paths of Glory* (1957), directed by Stanley Kubrick. The geography of the location is revealed in the wide shot at the end of the scene. Examine that image to get a feeling of the room and the actors' placement before exploring the rest of the shot positions in the overhead.

Paths of Glory tells the story of a regiment of French soldiers stationed on the German front in World War I. It is a study in the imbalance of power between the men who actually fight the war and those who make the decisions regarding how it will be fought. The generals are seen living in grand palaces as they decide the fate of soldiers who are dying in the trenches of the battleground.

The commanding officer orders his men to take a German position called "the ant hill." He knows that is an exceedingly difficult if not impossible task, but to further his own political ambitions he sends his men into the battle. They are mowed down before they even get to the German line, and the few survivors fall back into the trenches. Because they failed to achieve this impossible goal, the general orders one man from each group of soldiers to be tried for treason and cowardice. If convicted, they are to be executed.

This scene is from the court martial. Kubrick moves the camera from one subjective position to another, letting us share different points of view, from the defense attorney's desk to the jury box. The overhead diagram is marked with the placement of the few set pieces in the courtroom, the blocking of the characters, and the camera positions numbered in edited shot sequence.

SHOT #1 · SHOT #2A · SHOT #2B

SHOT #3C · SHOT #3B · SHOT #3A

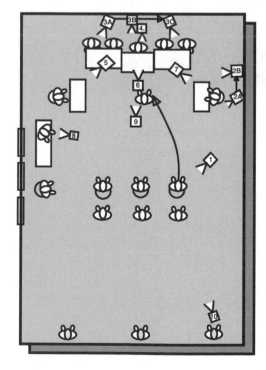

[continued on next page]

[*Paths of Glory*, 1957]
Trial sequence (partial): overhead diagrams of camera placement. Compare the
relationships of camera icons, as numbered, to film frames 1–10.

 SHOT #4

 SHOT #8

 SHOT #5

 SHOT #9

 SHOT #6

 SHOT #10

 SHOT #7

THE IMAGE

Storyboard images can come from various sources of inspiration. They can also be expressed in multiple ways. Whether you are an accomplished artist or someone struggling to draw a credible stick figure, there are many techniques that can help you express your vision.

Drawing

There are several highly technical methods to develop imagery these days, but most storyboard images are still created by the old-fashioned method; they're drawn using the familiar tools of paper, pencil, charcoal, and ink. These simple supplies and your mind are all that is necessary to express ideas about composition and camera position to yourself and your collaborators.

Unless you are interested in working as a professional illustrator (which requires a high level of proficiency), creating effective storyboards doesn't necessarily require great drawing skill. There are many simple approaches to drawing that can easily serve those of you who just need a tool for communication.

In the following chapters, the perspective and figure notation techniques that will be outlined will enable even a filmmaker with undeveloped drawing skills to sketch understandable, usable storyboard frames. A few days or even hours of investigation will reward you with expanded skills that will help you better communicate visual ideas.

INT. LIFEBOAT (MORNING) - TWO SHOT - KOVAC AND JOE

With all their strength they hold onto the sail rope. Back of them, in the sea, Stanley comes into the SHOT and Kovac rushes over to the side of the boat to haul him in. As he starts pulling on the rope:

[*Lifeboat*, 1943]
Director: Alfred Hitchcock

> "Close your eyes and visualize…"
> —Alfred Hitchcock

Photography, Video, and the Computer

I often take a digital camera with me when I accompany a director on location, and as I shadow the director and our collaborators, I constantly use the camera's zoom function to pop off shots that reference possible camera angles. Using a medium resolution to make the most of your memory card, you can later download the shots into a photo manipulation computer application, such as Photoshop, and then use these images as the base layer for a storyboard. Simply draw figures as another layer or print these images and use a light box to sketch the basic lines of the environment.

Another possibility is to use a video camera to record shot possibilities and then print screen grabs with a software program such as SnapNDrag that will allow you to select a frame and save it as a jpg or tiff file.

In Appendix I (page 218) you will find short reviews of a number of computer applications, some of which will allow you to add effects and transitions between shots, such as cross-dissolves or wipes, and then play your scene back in real time. Audio tracks can also be added to the storyboard to increase the presentation's appeal.

PUTTING IT ALL TOGETHER

Whether you choose to develop your imagery by high or low technical methods, keep in mind that the image must agree with the diagram, and they both must be in concert with the shot list. When all elements of the preproduction documents are in agreement, then the readers can easily move from the overhead to the image and from there to the shot list. They can, in fact, move in any order they care to and have each piece of information build onto the last, rather than having it cause confusion and additional questions.

Digital storyboard (detail) made with Poser and Photoshop

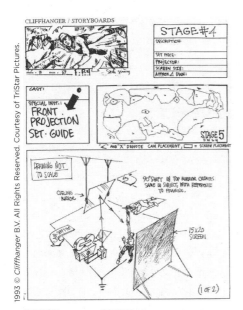

[*Cliffhanger*, 1993]
Drawing: John Mann

NUMBERING SYSTEM

Contemporary shooting scripts in the American film industry are broken down into individual scenes. Each time the script calls for a change in location, it will note that new location with a new scene number. Shots are numbered with a reference to the scenes that they appear in. Often the shot numbers are reset to "1" at the beginning of each scene so that you will have, for instance, Scene 5, shots 1-25; Scene 6, shots 1-26; Scene 7, shots 1-12, and so on. This method eliminates the need to renumber the storyboard if a scene happens to be cut.

The shots should be numbered so that each shot gets a separate designation. Shots that need more than one frame can be then sub-numbered with a lettering system, e.g., shot 5a, 5b, 5c, and so on. When you need to render a cutback, it is useful to just give it the same number that it used when it first appeared in the scene. This way, your storyboard will be numbered according to how many shots are planned rather than by how many cuts are envisioned in the edited sequence.

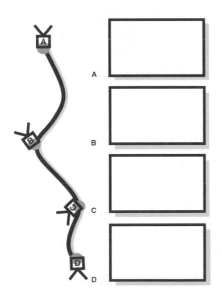

Digital storyboard (detail) made with Poser and Photoshop

SIDEBAR DIAGRAMS

There will be occasions when you plan a complex camera move and would like to include some additional information to clarify your intentions. A diagram included alongside the image can help to pinpoint your idea and eliminate the need to turn back to the overhead, which serves the entire sequence. Either in overhead or side view, this visual aid should have each position that is represented in the images marked with the image number. This way, even complicated Steadicam moves can be boarded using key frames for imagery and camera positions marked in a sidebar diagram for blocking.

"I was insecure at first (on *Boxcar Bertha*) because I had been fired from *The Honeymoon Killers* in 1968 after one week of shooting, and for a pretty good reason, too. It was a 200-page script and I was shooting everything in master shots with no coverage because I was an artist! ...Of course, not every scene was shot from one angle, but too many of them were, so there was no way of avoiding a film that was four hours long. That was a great lesson. From 1968 to 1972, I was very much afraid that I would get fired again. So when I started *Boxcar Bertha* I drew every scene, about 500 pictures altogether."

— Martin Scorsese
Scorsese on Scorsese

TEXT REFERENCES IN THE STORYBOARD

Along with having the shot list accompany the storyboard and overhead as a separate document, it is a good idea to transfer some or all of its information movement of a Steadicam shot onto the storyboard itself. This usually takes the form of blocks of text that appear beneath or alongside the image. Not having the best handwriting, I take a copy of the shot list, slice it up and then paste the corresponding shot description under each image. This looks neat and makes it easy for someone to find a particular image if they're reading the shot list and want to check an image out on the storyboard.

All of this is theoretical until you try it out yourself and see what works for you. The following exercise outlines a short, simple scene without dialogue, which you can use to practice these ideas.

EXERCISE: THE STORYBOARD MOMENT

An Exercise for Creating a Coordinated Shot List, Overhead Diagram, and Storyboard

For the following short scene, work out an overhead diagram, a shot list, and images for a 10-14 shot sequence. Mark the camera positions and character blocking on the overhead, and be sure to use the same aspect ratio for each of the frames.

1. Exterior, urban street. There is someone standing on a corner.

2. Across the street a door opens and a second person emerges.

3. The second person crosses the street to the first person.

4. They exchange something.

5. They leave, either together or apart.

Notice that the description lacks details. You need to add the story to this. Is it a Western? A film noir scene? A romantic comedy? Decide on the gender of the characters, the "something" that they exchange, and feel free to embellish the story's skeletal structure.

Have fun and don't worry about the drawing, just use this exercise to become familiar with the process of working from a shot list and overhead in planning your imagery.

A student example of the Storyboard Moment follows.

SHOT LIST, "THE STORYBOARD MOMENT"

#1   A frontal long shot of a man, "A." Man "A" is walking toward the camera.

#2   A frontal Med. low angle shot of a man, "B." A man who wears a nice suit is standing in front of a car.

#3   A POV of man "B." A frontal Med. eye level shot of man "A."

#4   A O.T.S. of man "A." A frontal long shot of man "B."

#5   Shot on a C.U. of man "B." As he turns his head, camera PAN right a little. End shot a C.U. of man "B."

#6   A frontal Med. shot of the signal light. Light changes from green to red.

#7   A frontal long low angle shot of a train. The train runs toward the camera.

#8   A O.T.S. of man "B." As the train runs across the frame, we cannot see man "A."

#9   A frontal wide low angle shot of the train. Camera PAN left to show a man in the train who wears a hat. He drops a bottle out of the window.

#10   Open shot on a wide rear 3/4 eye level angle of man "A." Man "A" watches the back of the train. On the right side, we can see man "B." Camera is TRAVELING to the back side of man "A." End shot on a O.T.S. of man "A." A frontal full figure of man "B."

#11   A frontal high angle of two shot of two men. Man "A" walks toward the camera.

#12   A frontal Med. angle of man "B." As man "A" walks into the frame from the right side, camera changes focus to man "A." End shot on a profile extreme C.U. of man "A."

#13   A frontal Med. shot of man "A." On the left side of frame, we also can see the long shot of man "B." Man "A" puts his left hand into his jacket.

#14   A frontal C.U. of man "A's" hand, which holds the bottle.

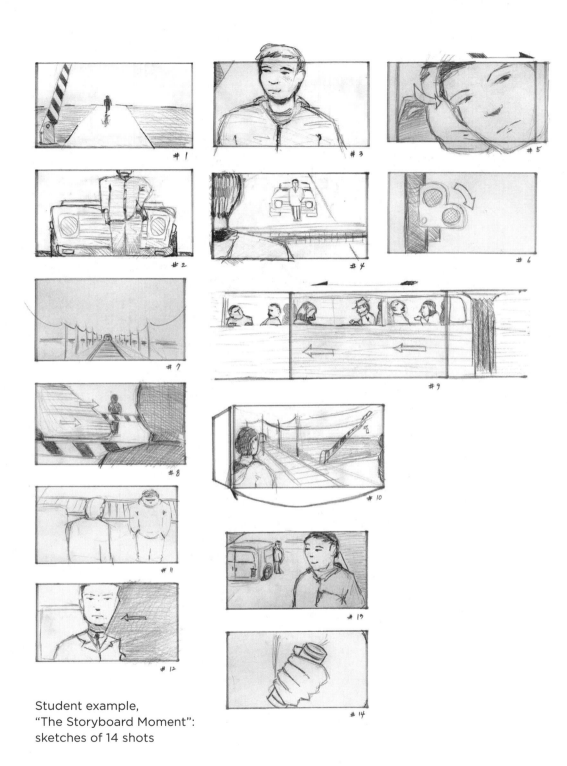

Student example,
"The Storyboard Moment":
sketches of 14 shots

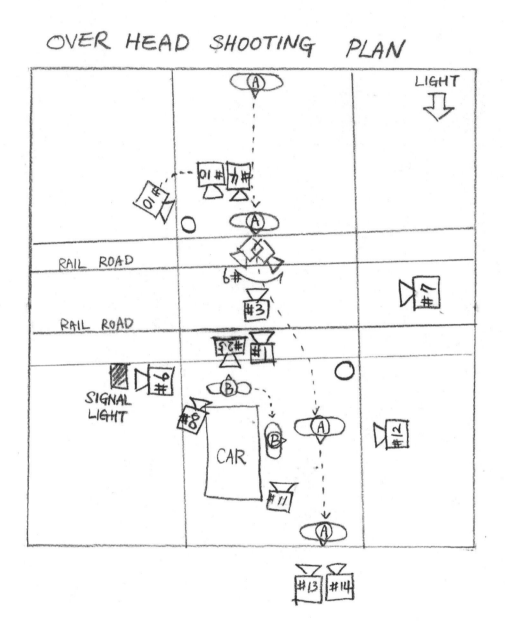

Student example,
"The Storyboard Moment
project": Roger Lee

SUMMING UP AND MOVING ON

This chapter has explored the interworkings of Text, Diagram, and Image in the process of preproduction visualization. Each element communicates information by a different method.

> The Text: a shot list that alludes to visual aspects of the frame in words, using a specific vocabulary.

> The Diagram: an overhead view of the set with camera positions and character blocking marked down using icons and arrows. This document is both abstract and concrete in its use of simplified forms and scale drawing.

> The Image: a drawing or photo-based image that describes the composition of the frame. The most concrete of all the storyboard documents, it shows the content of the shot in static or extended frames that refer to movement of the camera.

The next chapter will discuss aspect ratios and outline the technique of extended frames for shots that use a moving camera. The technique of extending frames to show camera movement is a contemporary development in the art of story-boarding that is surprisingly easy to master and adds dynamic movement to your project.

CINEMATIC DIRECTOR AT ELECTRONIC ARTS (EA)

On Games vs. Movies

"An audience member is a voyeur when watching a feature film. You may see the movie in a theater and then perhaps once again on DVD or cable, and that's it. But with a game controller in your hands, you are actively interacting with the story and the game play — you have to think; it's an entirely different experience than sitting passively in your theater seat. The majority of games that are made from features fail miserably because they are rushed into release with the movie. Games need to be vetted to ensure that they have first-rate game play; to a dedicated gamer, game play is far more important than the quality of the game's imagery. However, the most successful games are a combination of great game play and stunning imagery.

When a game requires exposition or story told throughout the game, this is done with cinematic sequences. These are non-interactive scenes (NIS) that play throughout the game. There's a script written after the design of the game is completed. The scriptwriters work with the game designers, art director, and cinematic director to ensure that all the elements have continuity. There's a massive amount of imagery and data that must be tracked and combined in real time by a game engine as a player moves through a game. This real-time interactivity is technically far more sophisticated than the process of creating special effects for a feature film.

On Process

Initially, I'm given an outline of the dramatic story and the game play. From the beginning of the process, the art director and the animation director are developing the environments and the main characters featured in the game. As we progress I'm given a more refined script and then begin to work with the art director on the specifics of the cinematic production. Occasionally the cinematic department will come up with ideas that are incorporated into the game play. Every game has an Executive Producer who, like a director in film, must coordinate the game's design, engineering, art, and cinematics.

Once I have the script I write down ideas and create thumbnail drawings in my sketchbook that break down the different sequences into shots. When I feel I'm on the right path, I scan the drawings and then edit them and move them around in Photoshop until I'm happy with a sequence. I then work with a storyboard artist to create more refined boards, and after that I write

[*Command &
Conquer*:
Red Alert 3, 2008]
Cinematic
storyboards
and game frames

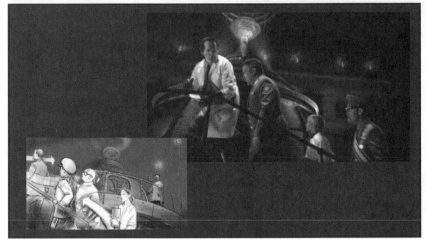

[*Command &
Conquer*:
Red Alert 3, 2008]
Green screen
pre-viz

17

Rear high angle coverage

3R

*The SD flies vertically up the
front of the Mech. The camera follows.*

scene descriptions on the individual frames. During this conceptual phase I use hundreds of reference stills gathered from a variety of sources and sometimes shoot stills to help define a shot. I've always believed that every shot and every sequence should have a beginning, middle, and end. The script is the trail we must follow. I try to make the trail emotionally involving, dramatic, and visually interesting.

I'm always thinking editorially and try to give the editor plenty of options and coverage. I cover each scene with a wide, medium, and tight shot of the action and shoot other details that help the editor use moments from different takes. The storyboard artists I work with know 3D programs like Google's SketchUp. We build a 3D set to work out camera choreography. I look at many Quicktimes to refine the shots.

The storyboard always goes through iterations as various executive reviews take place throughout the corporation. For budgeting and production planning I use the storyboards to define what will be CG (computer-graphic-based imagery), what will be green screen, and what kind of camera and lighting equipment will be needed for the stage shoot. All this is essential for keeping the stage shoot

Zelinsky is too late. Einstein begins to fade away.

FX begin.

CU Zelinsky: "No-o--o-o-o-oo-o-o-!!"

Einstein disappears.

We see a peaceful winter scene in the Ardennes Forest. A light snow falls as birds feed in the foreground.

A rumble is heard....snow starts to fall from the branches. The came shakes and the birds fly away. Suddenly breaking through the pines is a giant Soviet Apocalypse tank. The trees fly to the side as the giant tank crashes forward snow kicks up.

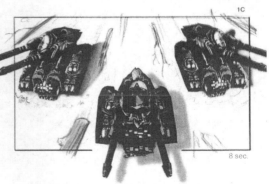

The tank breaks onto an open snow field free from the trees. The camera booms up and looks down as two other tanks move into the scene. The lead tank fires a shot.
We match cut to the next scene when the tank fires.

We see a view of the Roman Colosseum. In the foreground stands a Soviet Spider Walker with two pilots on board. The camera slowly pulls back.

*[Command & Conquer:
Red Alert 3*, 2008]
Director: Richard Taylor
Storyboards: Renee Reeser and David Duncan
Production Company: Electronic Arts
Sequence of storyboards created for the opening cinematic

on time and on budget, yet allowing room for change. No matter how well designed and planned it may be, the creative process must always allow for change. If I see that a shot isn't working, I'll come up with alternate solutions.

Usually I create an animatic from the storyboard frames. If a sequence has complex camera movement, I'll use the 3D elements created by the storyboard artist. Once the animatic is approved, depending on the budget of the game, we'll use it as a definitive guide to shooting. The color-coded board with written descriptions of the scenes, the animatic, and my director's overview are presented to outside contractors to bid on the work. Both live action production companies and computer animation studios bid cinematic sequences that entail live action production as well as high-end computer graphics. Once the job is awarded to a company, they create a 3D pre-viz of the entire board. The pre-viz clearly defines the staging of the live action scenes and the camera choreography of the CG scenes. Sequences that contain both live action and CG are usually composited internally and in some cases with another outside effects company.

On Developing Your Eye

I think learning to draw is essential to the creative process. You don't need to be a great artist, but a few drawings are, as it's often been said, worth a thousand words. Steven Spielberg does little thumbnail storyboard drawings that are quite simple, but they communicate how he wants to frame and stage a scene. Drawings solve problems and communicate ideas.

I believe that everyone in the creative arts should have a sketchbook or a journal to constantly document their ideas. Ideas need to be captured in some form or they are forgotten and fade away like dreams. I've kept journals for over 40 years, and I still refer to them daily for inspiration."

ON FINISH FETISH...

During my first few months in Los Angeles I was fortunate to get a call from the producer of the first feature on which I had been employed. He asked me if I was available to work on some concept sketches for a project that he was going to pitch at one of the major studios later that month. Although I had a full-time-plus job during the day I leapt at the chance to do some highly creative work. The film was to take place in a variety of locations, ranging from a Las Vegas rock-and-roll heaven to a post-apocalyptic, world-without-music hell. There was lots of room for embellishment. I worked nights and weekends, and when I showed the producer my ideas in rough-sketch form, he was delighted. I signed a development contract and was slated to accompany him to the meeting at Columbia Pictures.

Then I began to polish the rough sketches. I took all the drawings and had them transferred to heavy illustration board. Then I spent hours inking and coloring them in a tight, highly rendered style. I then mounted these paintings (they were no longer sketches) and placed them in a new, expensive portfolio I had purchased for my trip to Hollywoodland. Wrong. When I met with the producer a day before our scheduled meeting he took one look at the paintings (of which I was unashamedly proud) and shook his head. "I can't take these into the meeting," he said. "What happened to the drawings?"

I was barely breathing at this point. "I finished them," I offered.

"You killed them," he countered. "I'm pitching a treatment, not a finished project. These paintings make it seem that we've decided how the picture will look. I need to show them suggestions, get them interested in the project, not present them with a finished product."

And with a thanks and a handshake, that was the end of our alliance. The rough sketches had been sacrificed to the icon of tight beauty, and I'd lost out. (Then again, the project didn't get funded anyway, but that's not the point.) There are times when a loose sketch is simply more appropriate than a heavily rendered image. Knowing when to suggest a scene quickly rather than carve it out in stone will save you time and money in the end.

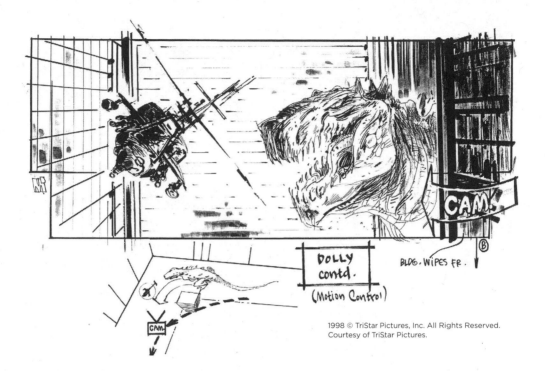

DOLLY contd.

(Motion Control)

BLDG. WIPES FR.

1998 © TriStar Pictures, Inc. All Rights Reserved.
Courtesy of TriStar Pictures.

Aspect ratio refers to the ratio between the horizontal and vertical dimensions of the screen. The aspect ratio of a project is determined by the medium. The width of the screen for film, television, and computers is always greater than the height.

"Godzilla's compositions are drawn so that they work in both 2:35 as well as 1:33. The director, Roland Emmerich, wanted to make sure that when this thing went to video it would look as good as possible. With the pan and scan technique sometimes the effects are shown off in a poor light, so he wanted to make the video look as exciting as the film. It's the first time I've ever been asked to work that way, and I think it's pretty inventive."

—John Mann
Illustrator: *Godzilla*,
1998

There are several standard aspect ratios in use today. They appear in ascending order of widths below:

TV OR COMPUTER SCREEN

TV or COMPUTER SCREEN
1.33:1   TV, computer screen, or pre-1952 American standard projection (also called 4:3 or Academy Standard)

16MM FILM OR EUROPEAN PROJECTION

16mm FILM or EUROPEAN PROJECTION
1.66:1   European standard and 16mm

AMERICAN PROJECTION

AMERICAN PROJECTION
1.85:1   American standard projection ratio, post 1950s

WIDESCREEN SUPER 35

WIDESCREEN SUPER 35
2.35:1   70mm, Widescreen, Cinerama, Cinemascope, and other super wide-screen formats

HIGH DEF

HIGH DEF
1.78:1 (also called 16:9)

IMAX

IMAX
1.43:1

FRAMING HISTORY

The 35-millimeter form was developed in the early 1890s by one of Edison's assistants, W. K. L. Dickson. The format began with a 35mm filmstrip 1-3/8" wide. There was an initial interest in creating a widescreen format, mostly from filmmakers who wanted to bypass Edison's patents and create their own technologies. The expense of this approach took its toll, and within a few years of its development, the 4:3 ratio had become the dominant format in the field, which remained largely unchanged for 60 years.

Before the advent of modern widescreen formats in the 1950s, there were isolated examples of filmmakers employing expanded techniques for certain sequences. Abel Gance's *Napoleon* (1927) used three synchronized cameras simultaneously in a system he called *Polyvision*. This process allowed him to create not only horizontal images with a ratio of 4:1, but also to use the elongated width to create montages of up to three images that appeared simultaneously on the screen.

As sound began to be incorporated into films, a new standard briefly appeared. The addition of a sound strip to the 35mm filmstrip in films during the 1926-27 season caused the image to be squeezed into the remaining area. That left a slightly taller format of 1.15 to 1 for the negative image, but it also resulted in an image loss of almost 25%. To compensate for this change in shape, some projectionists began to mask out the top and bottom of the film — essentially reformatting the image to fit the theater's existing projection screen. Amid the complaints of both audiences and technicians, the Academy of Motion Picture Arts and Sciences instituted a format known as the "Academy Aperture" in an effort to create an industry standard. This 1932 document restored the format of 1.33 (or a slightly expanded 1.37) to the industry, and it remained largely unrivaled until the rising popularity of television and its co-option of the 1.33 format 20 years later.

Since the introduction of television in the mid '50s, the 1.85:1 ratio has become the standard widescreen format for projected feature projects. The wider formats are still utilized in the Super 35, anamorphic, and 70mm shooting schemes.

THE RATIO AND THE MATERIAL

Deciding on the format in relationship to the necessities of the story

After a long reign as the ratio of choice, the "golden rectangle" began to disappear and the era of the epic widescreen frame appeared with a new, expanded horizon. The advent of such systems as Cinerama and CinemaScope in the early 1950s forever changed the experience of the audience and the canvas of the filmmaker. Instead of the slightly inflated square of 1.33 to 1, the new standard for film stretched this format into an extremely elongated rectangle of up to 2.77 to 1 (for Cinerama), almost double the area of the original frame.

One of the first decisions regarding the visualization of a film is the choice of its aspect ratio. Widescreen creates a heightened sense of audience participation and adds an epic scope to the storytelling. Although the standard projection frame is now 1.85:1, there are specific stories that call for a different format. Recent productions that rely heavily on special effects and large action sequences have adopted the super widescreen rectangle that was so prominent in the 1950s. Summer blockbuster entertainment such as *Moulin Rouge*, *Jurassic Park*, and *Titanic* have all been shot with the expanded ratios and make use of the added frame space to pull the audience into the spectacle of their environments.

Current independent films often focuses on stories that stress relationships and character development. These films are often shot in the prevailing 1.85:1 ratio and in addition are projected in 1.66:1 when they are shown in Europe, where they have a wide audience. The 1.85 format was agreed upon as a default compromise when the size of the movie audience continued to shrink with the advent of commercial television. As widescreen became a more familiar experience, the viewing public cooled a bit to its charms and chose to take their entertainment from the more convenient box in their living rooms. In addition, the movie palaces began to give way to shopping mall multiplexes and the size of the screen shrank accordingly. Even films that were shipped with the intention of a 2.35 release format were sometimes shown in 1.85 or even 1.66 to fit the screens of the newly reduced theaters. The newest format can be found in HDTV media, which has made 16:9 video (also called 1.78:1) the new widescreen video standard.

In keeping with the technical realities of the situation, producers reacted by shipping films that were intended to be viewed in this new standard, the widescreen as redefined by its relationship to television. In fact, the ultimate destiny of most films is the 1:33 format of the small screen. Today movies are shot with an eye to the composition of both the original frame and the ultimate frame that will be imposed by television. A "safe action area" has been added to the viewfinders of cameras so that the cinematographers can protect their compositions for the eventual release to other media.

COMPUTING THE ASPECT RATIO OF THE STORYBOARD

Aspect ratio is determined by the relationship of the height of the frame to its width. The height is described by the numeral one. The width is then written as a multiple of the height. The aspect ratio of a storyboard should match the dimensions of the medium it will be released in. So if you're working in television, you need to compose your shots in a 1.33:1 drawing. A convenient size is the 4" by 3" frame, stacked vertically so that you can fit three frames on an 8-1/2" by 11" standard-size sheet of paper. For a film shooting in 16mm, use the 1.66:1 version, which translates into a 5" by 3" frame. And for the Academy standard frame of 1.85:1, the size will work out to 5-1/2" by 3". These are just suggestions, as some directors prefer to work with only one image per page, while others choose to work from thumbnail sketches that might number up to 15 on a standard-size sheet.

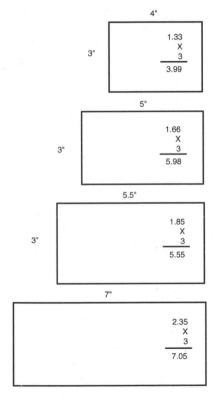

Examples of
Aspect Ratio Calculation

To calculate a correctly proportioned frame, start with the size of paper you'll be working with. You can orient the sheet either vertically or horizontally, but take into account that the script is a vertical document, and you might want to place the boards inside it or copy them on the reverse side of the script pages. Next, decide on how many frames you would like on one sheet of paper. Once you've settled on a height for the frame, let's say 4", multiply it by the aspect ratio of your media.

For example, if you're working on a picture shot in Cinemascope, then the width of the frame will be 2.35 times the height. Multiply 4 x 2.35 and you arrive at the width of the frame, which will be approximately 9.4". This method will give you the general storyboard dimension for your project.

TV FORMATTING: CHANGES TO THE ORIGINAL FRAME

Letterboxing

In recent years, with the popularity of cable stations that are aimed toward an audience of film purists, the practice of letterboxing films for television is becoming more common. The letterbox presents the film in its original format, with a black border filling the unused space at the top and bottom of the TV frame. This allows the entire width of a 1.85 or a Cinemascope film to be shown, while the height of the frame is reduced to only a portion of the television screen. Many DVD titles specialize in releasing letterbox versions of new and classic films, a format popularized earlier by the laserdisc. Please refer to Appendix I (page 218) for a list of DVDs that includes storyboards.

Pan-and-Scan

This is an alternative to the method of letterboxing and refers to a reformatting of the original composition. The pan-and-scan technology selects sections of imagery from the projection version and plugs them into the target aspect ratio, usually the 1.33:1 of television. This technique seeks to follow the action around the frame and will often result in cutting out secondary pieces of visual information that were crucial to the balance and meaning of the original composition. At its worst, the pan-and-scan method leaves little more than half of the frame and is a shadow of the filmmaker's original vision.

SUMMARY

It is imperative that when you work on preproduction visualization, you create frames that accurately reflect the intended aspect ratio of your project. Whether you are working in video or Cinemascope, the format offers you specific challenges in composition and framing. If you have the luxury of choosing among formats, then viewing films or videos using letterboxed examples can help you to decide which one will best serve your project. These films can also be excellent sources for ideas on composition and camera movement.

SET HARASSMENT

I was standing off camera watching a scene being shot. The director called "cut" and as the leading man walked past, he grabbed me and proceeded to give me a very wet and unwanted kiss on the lips.

I was shocked. I had spoken to this man a couple of times, but his advance was completely unexpected and not in the least romantic. This was only my second film and I was an assistant to the production designer. In other circumstances I might have let my outrage show, but in that situation my career seemed on the line. So, what do you do? Keep your mouth literally and figuratively shut? Or raise a stink and demand an apology from the actor and/or the producing organization? Tough call.

The gender split on the set seems to run about 1 to 10 in favor of the guys. Great odds if you're a woman looking to hook up with someone, but a difficult split if you are interested in some workplace peace and privacy. For anyone considering an on-set career, the handling of advances on the set can be an issue to consider.

Humor can be a great ally. You will be working in tight quarters and for long hours with the rest of the cast and crew. Having a few good brush-off lines that show you can be a good sport while placing limits on your availability will come in handy. If the gentleman persists in unwanted or crude remarks, then a private chat, out of earshot of the rest of the crew, might do the trick. The get-the-girl atmosphere that is sometimes fostered on sets can carry a sense of sport about it, and no one wants to be rebuffed in front of colleagues.

A straight, serious request for professional behavior presented with a no-hard-feelings attitude will often lighten the mood. It can calm down a situation that can otherwise be detrimental both to getting the job done and to enjoying it.

I kept my mouth shut about the actor's errant tongue and was plagued with invitations to his trailer and calls at home. It was clear to me that he was after a quick, uncomplicated encounter and was using his position to force the point. I am not proud of my handling of this situation. I kept my mouth shut, just smiled at him, and tried to steer clear of his path. After the show wrapped, I finally got around to telling him to leave me alone.

The imbalance of power in these types of situations can be unnerving. In a freelance business, one nasty outburst can haunt you for years. It takes practice, but standing up for your personal rights with a sense of humor and forgiveness can have a long-lasting effect on your relationship to the job and your coworkers.

2-4

TILT W/
TOM TOM

Storyboard by John Coven © 1998 Road Movies GMBH

"I'll often use extended frames for tracking shots, panning shots, and tilting shots. Sometimes I use the entire vertical length of the page for a craning shot. You need to be able to communicate the entire shot in that one image. The dimension that you have in film that you don't have in illustration is time. The art of storyboarding is in choosing the right moment of time for illustration. You need to be able to communicate the entire shot in that one image."

—John Coven
Illustrator: *The Usual Suspects*, *X-Men*

INTRODUCTION TO EXTENDED FRAMES

This chapter aims to familiarize you with the idea of extended frames. The extended frame format allows the storyboard artist to reference the time and space elements of filmmaking. The frame of film or television media is defined by its aspect ratio. This shape contains the visual information for a single, static shot. The single image held in this frame can only express one moment, a fraction of the time that the shot will actually last. One question that often comes up in the study of storyboarding is which moment to represent when you only have this single reference to the proposed shot.

To find the answer, it is useful to imagine how the shot begins and how it ends, and ask yourself: What are the important visual changes that occur between these two points? Perhaps someone enters the frame, or an argument breaks out and the shot covers some of the action. In these two circumstances you would want to focus on the large movements in the shot. For example, the moment a new character enters the frame, represent the movement with an arrow coming from outside the frame. On the other hand, visualizing a moment in the heat of the argument would give you an opportunity to create a composition that takes advantage of the emotion and action of the scene.

If you are an accomplished illustrator, then using forced perspective in a shot that includes active blocking can help to give the viewer a sense of the excitement and deep cinematic space. If your drawing skills are more modest, then go for a general sense of the scene's blocking. A well-placed arrow can tell your collaborators what you have in mind even if the details are broad and general. Again, focus on visualizing the starting and ending points of the shot, and then determine if you can express what you need the shot to do in one frame.

If you need more than one image to accomplish this, then one option is to create images that express two or more key frames of the shot.

The chapter will cover the following camera movements:

> Static

> Pan, Track, Swish Pan (horizontal shots)

> Tilt, Boom, Vertical Pan (vertical shots)

> Dolly (in/out), Zoom (in/out)

> Crane

> Zolly (zoom with counter dolly)

> Specialty moves, such as the handheld shot and the Steadicam

THE FRAME AS AN ICON OF MOVEMENT

Imagine a storyboard frame as a moving entity. The frame represents the picture plane of the camera. When you want to communicate the imagery seen by the camera's moving viewpoint, you can utilize one of two methods. You can draw, in separate frames, what the shot will look like at the start of the move and what it will look like after the move is over. This will give you two static representations of what the audience will see.

The second choice is to extend the edges of the frame to encompass the scope of the entire shot. If the camera is to travel the length of a room, for example, and the visual content of the shot changes completely from the start to the finish, then the aspect ratio of the shot can be doubled on the horizontal axis. If the camera rotates in a 270-degree arc, the triple width might be needed to show the entire breadth of information. You only need to extend the frame to include the visual information within the camera move. Sometimes this will be only a small amount, as in a shot that adjusts to the movement of a character with a subtle tilt and panning motion. In this case you might just use two slightly overlapping frames to get your point across.

[*The Cotton Club*, 1984]
Illustrator: Harold Michelson

Both methods are acceptable. You might opt for the second version and use extended frames when the sequence you are planning has many camera moves. The pages will be more dynamic in design and show the camera's movement more fluidly. The static method, using individual frames of the same size and shape, can be used when you need to save time and print out sheets of frames in advance.

I often use my computer to print the storyboard frames. I have stored files with frames of different aspect ratios and various extended frame shapes. When I have a shot list ready, I print out the number of static frames needed, the extended frames that are already stored, and then create any new frame shapes that are necessary. Next to each frame I have a text box printed to hold the shot list information.

In addition, it is useful to design a place on the sheet for the shot and scene numbers. It is easier to read the board if you are consistent with the placement of each item of information. If you place the scene number on the top right of the first sheet, continue the practice for every scene that you board. The shot numbers should be close to the frames, and in most cases the numbering system for each scene will start from the number one. This way, if a scene is omitted, the missing section will not throw off the numbering sequence.

In the pages that follow, you will find various examples of frame extensions and explanations of the camera movements that motivate them. As you examine each frame, understand that the camera movement being illustrated is only one example of that particular move. If the camera is booming and tracking, then the combination of frames that stack vertically as well as horizontally will be needed, but there are many different combinations that can be formed using this basic concept.

At the end of this section an exercise called "The Single Image Storyboard" will lead you through a storyboard sequence created with a single photo image. This will allow you to practice the technique of creating extended frames without being concerned about drawing interior imagery. This technique can only be mastered by hands-on use, so begin to experiment with it on your next sequence of shots. Your board will be a more dynamic expression of the film or video that is yet to come.

STATIC FRAME AND ADDITIONAL INFORMATION
FOR THE STORYBOARD PAGE

LOCATION, SCENE #

SHOT #

TEXT BOX: CAN BE USED TO TRANSFER SHOT LIST INFORMATION INTO THE STORYBOARD.

HORIZONTAL MOVEMENT

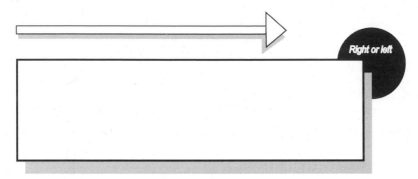

Panning or Tracking on the horizontal plane

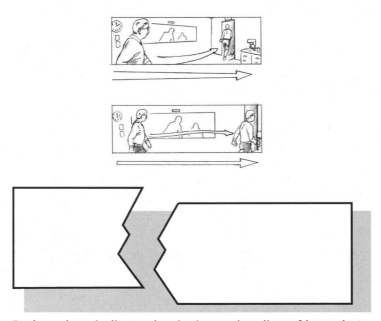

Broken plane indicates beginning and ending of long shot

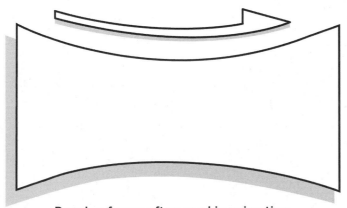

Panning frame often used in animation

VERTICAL MOVEMENTS
BOOM OR VERTICAL PAN (TILT)

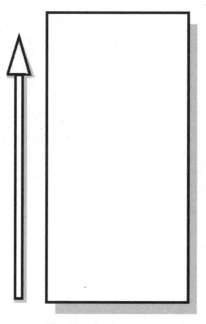

Tilt, Vertical Pan or Boom

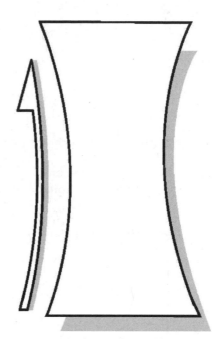

Alternate profile

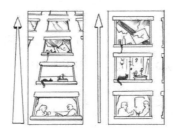

MOVEMENT ON THE VERTICAL AND HORIZONTAL AXES

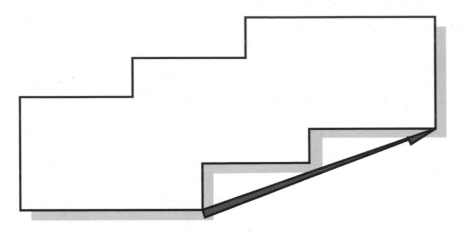

Pan or Track with a Tilt or Dolly
(Vertical and horizontal movement at the same time)

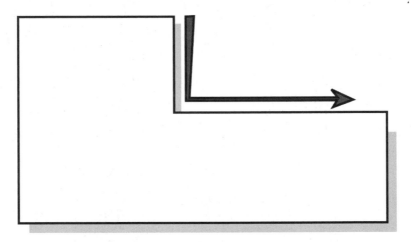

Tilt/Boom down and then Pan/Track screen left

COMBINATION OF MOVEMENT
IN/OUT AND UP/DOWN

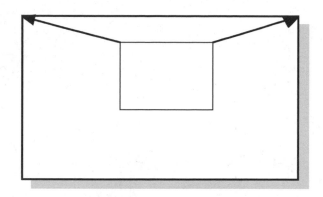

Dolly back or Zoom out
(Dolly or Zoom in by changing direction of arrows)

Dolly or Push-in to follow

THREE-WAY MOVEMENT OVER, UP OR DOWN AND IN AND OUT

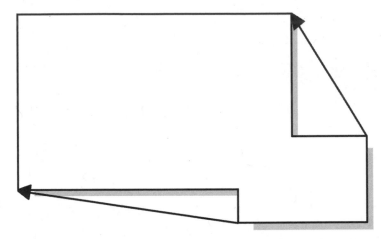

Dollying or Zooming out, Panning or Tracking to the left and Booming or Tilting up

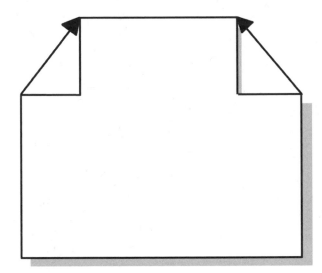

Dolly/Zoom in and Tilt or Boom up. Can reverse arrows for moves out.

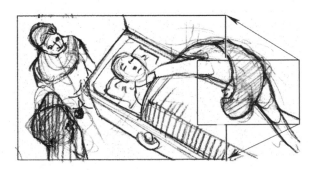

MOVEMENT IN THE DEPTH OF THE FRAME

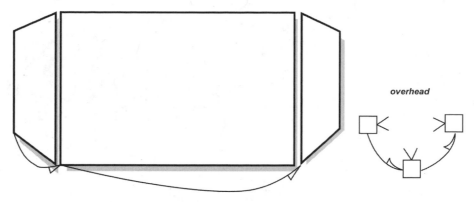

overhead

Semi-circular Track with Counter-pan

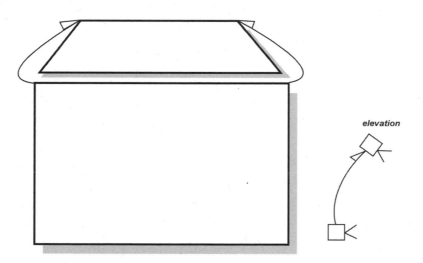

elevation

Crane up and over

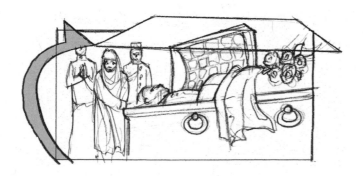

CRANES AND CIRCULAR TRACKING SHOTS

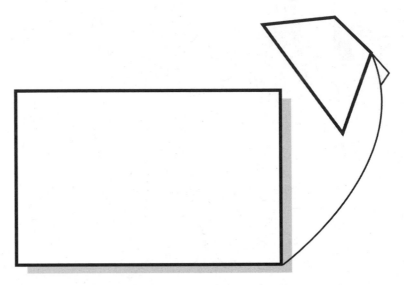

Crane up and to the right, Tilt down to keep action centered

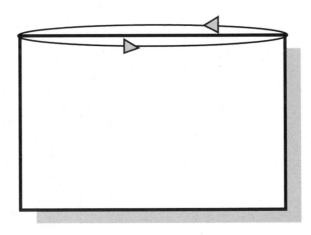

360-degree Pan

SPECIALTY MOVES

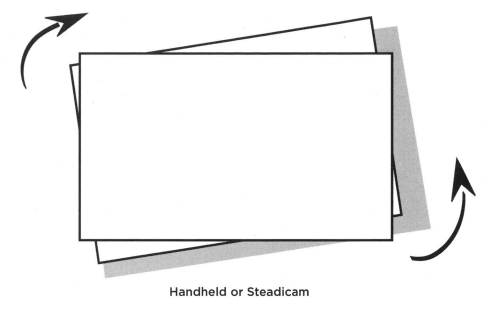

Handheld or Steadicam

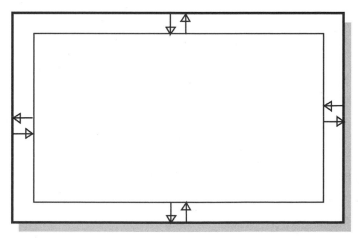

Zolly, aka Dolly with a Counter Zoom

STEADICAM AND LENGTHY HAND-HELD MOVEMENT

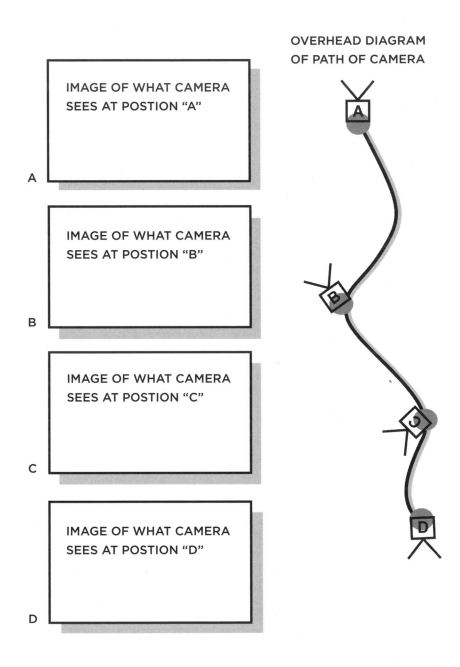

OVERHEAD DIAGRAM
OF PATH OF CAMERA

IMAGE OF WHAT CAMERA
SEES AT POSTION "A"

A

IMAGE OF WHAT CAMERA
SEES AT POSTION "B"

B

IMAGE OF WHAT CAMERA
SEES AT POSTION "C"

C

IMAGE OF WHAT CAMERA
SEES AT POSTION "D"

D

EXERCISE:
THE SINGLE IMAGE STORYBOARD

The following exercise offers an opportunity to practice using extended frames. It also can give you a good workout in editing.

1. Choose an image. It can be a photo, painting, or tapestry, just as long as it has good narrative content. The best images have a good mix of foreground, mid-ground, and background elements.

2. Create multiples of the image, either on a copying machine or in a computer application that allows image manipulation, such as Adobe Photoshop.

> "The Japanese approach drawing from quite a different direction than our method. They take an image of the branch of a cherry tree. The pupil cuts out from this whole, with a square, and a circle, and a rectangle: compositional units. He frames a shot!"
>
> — Sergei Eisenstein "Cinematographic Principle and the Ideogram," *Film Form,* 1929

3. Using a consistent aspect ratio, crop out various shots from the whole. Try to find 8 to 14 shots, and have at least four that use a moving camera.

4. Arrange the "shots" onto paper and experiment with various arrangements.

5. Paste in place and add arrows where needed. Don't add text; this is a "silent" film.

6. Show the sequence to a group and ask someone to talk their way through the narrative.

For an extra challenge, try to make the sequence tell a different story than the original image does.

SINGLE IMAGE STORYBOARD EXAMPLE: "TIJUANA RALLY"

1.

2.

← PAN LEFT

3.

STATIC

4.

STATIC

5.
DOLLY
OUT

6.
STATIC

7.
BOOM
UP

8.
TILT
DOWN

PAN
LEFT

9.
DOLLY
RIGHT

10.
STATIC

VICE PRESIDENT OF CREATIVE DEVELOPMENT AT PLATINUM STUDIOS

On Content Development

"We are unique in the way we develop content. Working on simultaneous development, we need to approach our creative process outside the traditional silo of much corporate structure. A big component of what we do here is create art that is participatory, something that the audience can have a hand in. Web comics can be flexible in that way, as we create so quickly that there can be almost immediate responses in the content development. If our audience gets ahead of the story we can, in a matter of days or even hours, make changes if it's called for in the story.

We encourage makers to think of themselves as creating worlds rather than single ideas. Also, nothing great is created by committee. We believe in the concept of authors. The individual vision is so important to us. We use email, Skype, whatever is available to keep in touch with our creative teams around the world. I can't tell you how many executives from big studios are coming to us and asking for fully fleshed-out worlds that many people can play in, rather than high-concept pitches.

On Process

We usually start a comic book or graphic novel project from a basic concept, which often comes to us in the form of an oral pitch. Then we develop the key visual art, because that work informs where the script will go. It's a simultaneous process. The art informs the story and the story informs the art, because the creative work is a true amalgamation of both words and images.

In a traditional film project you would work from concept to script to visuals, but we work from concept to conceptual art to script, then back to art. And even once the art is completed, it may re-inform the storytelling to the point that we go back and rewrite the script. Then again, sometimes the story looks great in script form, but when we go to the visuals we need to cut things and move them around — much like the editing process.

We work on simultaneous platforms: when we start a project, we think about how it may affect our film division and television division. We try to work on projects that will have a life in all media platforms. For instance, a current project, *Hero By Night*, came from an outside creator and was acquired through our yearly competition. The story follows a boy who discovers the lair of a superhero who had disappeared in the 1950s. Among the artifacts he finds are journals that had been written by the hero, and for our web component, we created journal pages that were posted months before the actual comic landed in the stores. One journal page a day, created by the original artist and a small support team, went up on the web. We also created online avatars and merchandise as well as pitched the project for film and television projects.

On Style

When we start on a project, we consider what visual style will suit the content. How does the art itself express the world and the genre of this world? There is more variety in animation and comics than in live action film. We think about what the reader is going to respond to on an instinctual level if they are just looking at the art. A simple story needs a simple visual style. What do we want people to react to on a visual level — that leads us to decisions on that style.

One of our most successful titles is *Men in Black*. In that project, the style and tone of the art greatly influenced the tone of the movie. The original art was black and white and so simple in form that you could barely tell the difference between the two main characters, because that was the essence of who they were — they worked together as a unit. That translated into the movie's story arc, which covered their learning to work together as that unit. The visualization of the comics medium informed what the director eventually decided to do with the style of the film."

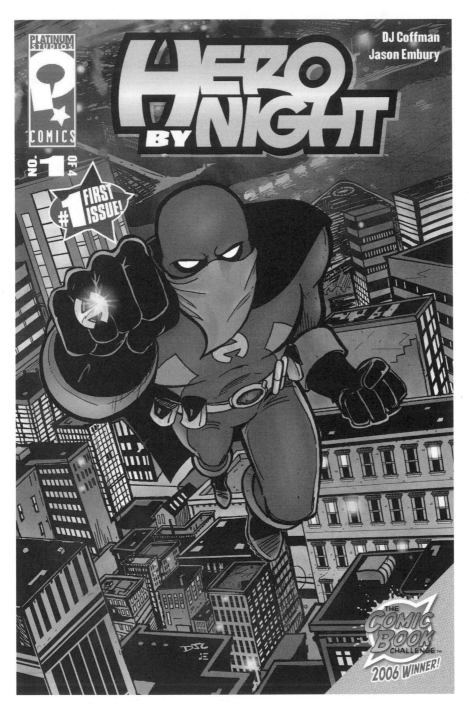

[*Hero By Night*]
Cover of published comic

[*Hero By Night*]
Web comic

[*Hero By Night*]
Video game

[*Hero By Night*]
Web journal

"I'll often use extended frames for tracking shots, panning shots, and tilting shots. Sometimes I use the entire vertical length of the page for a craning shot. You need to be able to communicate the entire shot in that one image. The dimension that you have in film that you don't have in illustration is time. The art of storyboarding is in choosing the right moment of time for illustration. You need to be able to communicate the entire shot in that one image."

—John Coven
Illustrator: *The Usual Suspects, X-Men*

In Conclusion

Scott McCloud, author of *Reinventing Comics*, has a concept called the 'infinite canvas,'*which refers to the possibilities for a digital, virtual space and how its expansion affects the creative possibilities of online and other content. It's so easy these days to create content — with a computer and some consumer level software almost anyone can. At Platinum we are looking to blur the lines between creator and audience."

*For more information please see
scottmccloud.com/4-inventions/canvas/index.html

I WANT IT CHEAP, FAST, AND UGLY

I was called in for an interview to storyboard an episode of an hour-long dramatic series for ABC. This was a fairly unusual request, because most episodic dramas have very short preproduction schedules. For that reason, as well as financial concerns, most of these series forego the storyboarding process.

This particular show had some unique challenges. They explained to me that most of the episode was to take place on a bridge at night. And a portion of the story took place on top of that bridge. The production manager had estimated that they would need five days to shoot the bridge sequences. The problem was, they were only able to secure the location, a bridge in downtown Los Angeles, for a single night.

The production designer planned to build a full-size model of the lower portion of the bridge in a parking lot at the studio. Then, on one of the stages, the top of one of the bridge's arches would be constructed. They needed to storyboard to plan out which shots had to be accomplished at the original location, which could be taken on the parking lot set, and finally, what needed to be done on the stage set.

The producer and director took a look at my portfolio and asked when I could start the project, as shooting was scheduled for the next week. I agreed to start immediately, and then the producer asked if he could speak with me privately for a moment. (Watch out for this one, my mother's voice whispered in my head.) When we were alone in his office, the producer closed the door. He walked over to me and said in a soft, intense voice, "I want them fast, I want them cheap, and I don't care if they're pretty."

He wanted the job done and me out of there as soon as possible. Only in the most dire of circumstances would this producer agree to hire an illustrator. And he didn't want the clock ticking his dimes away for any longer than was absolutely necessary. I called my assistant and we hammered out close to 150 frames in the next three days. I delivered the project by the weekend and they were pretty, in spite of it all. No extra charge.

[*Lifeboat,* 1944]

INTRODUCTION

There are two ways of viewing a film: passively and actively. The passive viewer sits back and enjoys the show, rarely asking why particular choices of composition or camera placement have been made. The active viewer not only sees and hears the film, but also is involved in exploring it on a deeper level — one that is not immediately apparent to the casual viewer.

Elements such as the color of the setting, the movement of the camera, and the position of objects or placement of people within the frame are experienced on a subconscious level. Sometimes this information is recognizable on the first viewing (especially if you are an active

"I never look through the camera, you know. When in doubt I draw a rectangle then draw the shot out for [the cameraman]. The point is that you are, first of all, in a two-dimensional medium. Mustn't forget that. You have a rectangle to fill. Fill it. Compose it."

—Alfred Hitchcock

viewer and pay attention to these details), but it often requires a second or third viewing to see past the action and dialogue in a film and pick up the subtleties of its visual storytelling.

By taking an active role you can begin to participate in the thought processes and active decisions that are used to form the work of art. Once you have learned how to actively observe, you will find that in addition to enjoying the film as entertainment, you will be investigating each image as an expression of the narrative. The graphic, two-dimensional structure of the frame is a powerful medium of communication. A great deal can be absorbed by looking at the various ways that directors, cinematographers, and art directors can manipulate the composition of the frame to maximize its use as a strong storytelling device. This chapter will cover different approaches to breaking down the frame and its composition into their component design parts and investigating how decisions of line, form, depth, and texture affect the "read" of the picture.

The first section will explore the relationship between composition and story. The narrative structure of a film and the atmosphere and tone of its story can be read in its images as well as the dialogue and action. Visual choices affect the way the audience understands the characters and their surroundings. Different approaches to composing the frame such as the use of open versus closed framing and other practices will be explored, along with ideas on positive and negative space and other fundamentals of composition.

The rest of the chapter will focus on the formal aspects of design as it applies to the film and video frame — including graphic composition as expressed in strategies of symmetry, balance, and randomness, among many others. The qualities of value, contrast, and texture will be covered as well.

[*October,* 1928]
Example of randomness

One note of caution: There can be a tendency toward trying to create a design template for the purpose of expressing story and character through imagery. Beware! Looking for absolute meanings to attach to specific camera angles or colors can be misleading. Each shot must be considered in the light of what has come before it and what is to come after it. It is the context that imparts meaning, not a slavish adherence to formulas.

COMPOSITION:
FORMAL CONSIDERATIONS IN THE DESIGN OF THE FRAME

Overview of Chapter: The Frame

> Positive and Negative Space

> Depth cues

> Overlap, focus, scale

> Symmetry

> Balance

> Series

> Randomness

> Shape

> Circle, arc, square, triangle, spiral, rectangle, linear

> Diagonal, horizontal, vertical

> Texture

> Contrast, value

> Framing devices

> Open and closed framing

THE FRAME

Our world has an endless horizon. Look up, down, turn in any direction and you are met with a seamless cyclorama of imagery. The frame is a tool that we use to break up this panorama into digestible pieces. The frame is a cropping device that snips away what we, as designers and directors, do not want the audience to see. The audience can be placed in a unique relationship with a character or environment through the specificity of these choices. The possibilities are limitless.

The manipulation of point of view is a powerful aspect of storytelling that is played out in the placement of objects and/or people inside the frame. The frame is a mobile window that can open onto any section of a scene, at any distance we desire. Because of this mobility, we can present the world with a more precisely composed structure than we usually encounter in our everyday lives. The camera can structure images of the world that are remarkable in their symmetry or randomness, their balance or internal geometry. Before exploring the specifics of these compositional strategies, there are a few general topics of two-dimensional design that need to be introduced.

POSITIVE AND NEGATIVE SPACE

There is a well-known illusion in which, while a person gazes at a drawing of a candlestick, it seems to transform into a double portrait. Using a contour that can be read in two ways to separate the black and white areas of the frame creates the illusion. The eye reads the white area as an object and sees the image as a candlestick, or favors the dark areas and sees them as silhouetted profiles.

[*October,* 1928]
Example of positive and negative space

This perceptual trick illustrates the play of positive and negative space. Positive space in a composition is an area that defines an object or figure. It is form. Negative space is that area which defines the space around these forms. Both spaces require a designing eye, but often the negative space is ignored, considered to be somehow less important than the positive space in frame composition.

In fact, they are locked together in a dance of mutual support. A shot of an apple sitting on a table is as much about the atmosphere around the apple as the apple itself. And aside from aesthetic considerations, the negative space can also hold the possibility of movement, surprise, or danger coming from outside the frame. The examples of film frames in this chapter highlight the various approaches to composition.

DEPTH IN THE FRAME

Depth within the frame is illusory. The frame or screen is a flat form; the depth we perceive is a result of fooling the eye — we believe that we see a third dimension where there is none. There are a number of visual cues that the eye and mind recognize as references to depth:

> A change in scale

> Overlapping objects

> Changes in focus or depth of field

> Color shifts

These visual cues imply the existence of a space beyond the screen. Learning to recognize and use them offers expanded control over the visual construction of each shot.

CHANGE IN SCALE

A friend of mine was working as a set dresser on a feature being produced in Los Angeles. One day during preproduction, the set decorator gave him a list of items to round up for the next set. My friend noticed a large array of children's items on the list, from clothes to outdoor furniture to tiny lighting fixtures. He was confused. There were no children in the script. Could the designer be padding the shopping list with objects he needed for his own home?

The answer came the next day when they arrived at the set, which was built on a soundstage. Most of the story they were filming took place in a New York apartment and its rear courtyard. In order to make the most of the limited stage space, the production designer designed the "buildings" surrounding the "yard" to 1/2 and 1/4 scale. The little clothes and furniture were to grace the balconies and windows of the scaled-down buildings, which through the camera appeared to be in perfect proportion and a great distance away.

3/4-SIZE BUILDINGS   1/2-SIZE BUILDINGS ACROSS YARD   FULL-SIZE BUILDING

[*Queens Logic,* 1988]
Production designer: Edward Pisoni

Raise your hand up so that it is positioned about 12 inches from your face. Now look beyond your hand to some architectural element in the room or on the street outside a window. Notice the relative size of your hand to the wall or the door. There is a severe diminishing of perceived size as an object recedes into the distance.

Art directors can use this knowledge to fool the eye into thinking that a set is much larger than it truly is. If you build a wall in the distance at half scale, the audience will "read" the wall as being much farther away. Increase the scale and the eye will tell the brain that the wall is much closer. Place a tall actor in the middle ground of a composition and a shorter actor's head in the foreground will be even with his.

[*Alexander Nevsky,* 1938]

[*M, 1931*]

OVERLAPPING OBJECTS

An infant thinks that when her mother disappears into the next room, she no longer is part of the world. Through repeated experience the child learns that out-of-sight does not mean out-of-existence. We grow and begin to know the world in more explicit ways, and the sight of a body partially hidden by a piece of furniture does not panic us into calling 911 for fear that the body has somehow lost its legs. We learn early on that appearances are deceiving, and the image of one object obscuring another is interpreted as a spatial cue.

In film, overlapping objects occur when the camera is positioned so that one form partially obscures another. When you raise or lower the camera, more of the hidden object will come into view. Our eyes judge distance and depth by the density of the superimposed items and the amount of visual information that is hidden.

CLOSE-UP WITH WIDE LENS BEFORE ZOLLY

CLOSE-UP WITH LONG LENS AFTER ZOLLY

CHANGE IN FOCUS AND DEPTH OF FIELD

Focus and depth of field are a function of the lens length and the aperture used during exposure of the film. A shot with a narrow field of focus can emphasize a figure, for example, by throwing the surrounding environment into an indistinct haze. This forces the audience to concentrate on one plane of space while de-emphasizing the remaining depth of the frame. Using a wide-angle lens will offer a much deeper depth of focal plane and integrate the object into its environs. A change in focus during a shot, a rack focus, leads the audience's eye through the frame by changing the plane of focus as they watch.

Another, though less common, use of depth of field can be found in the zolly, or zoom-with-a-counter-dolly shot. In this camera move, the characters or object being viewed will often stay the same relative scale while the lens length changes. The scale is maintained by the movement of the camera on a dolly that counters the zooming activity of the lens. The composition does change, though, as seen in the following examples.

COMPOSITIONAL STRATEGIES

Film and video are media that primarily use representative imagery to tell their stories. But we can also look to abstract design principles for ways to move the eye around the frame. Each frame or shot can be composed according to one or more two-dimensional design strategies. Even so-called "random" or "documentary-style" setups can be devised using these compositional structures.

SYMMETRY

A symmetrical frame is one that is always balanced: For every form and line on one side of the frame, there is a corresponding form or line on the opposite side. Symmetry is also characterized by an "angle of reflection." This angle is an imaginary line that runs through the frame and separates the two mirror-image halves vertically, horizontally, or diagonally.

Angle of reflection

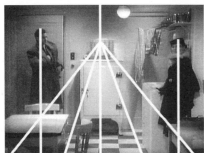

The symmetry of one-point perspective

There is also a type of symmetry that is known as "radial symmetry," where rather than a line of reflection, the symmetry is constructed around a center point. Forms that radiate out from a pivotal spot create balance.

A one-point perspective setup often creates a symmetrical frame automatically. When the camera's picture plane is parallel to the set and the camera is positioned in a central place relative to a wall or a street, the resulting frame will often have a strong symmetrical element.

ASYMMETRY

The asymmetrical frame is more than a frame that simply lacks absolute symmetry. It has, as an overriding aspect of its design, a variety of forms placed without regard to any mirroring plan.

[*M*, 1931]

BALANCE

In the three-dimensional world, balance is a matter of physical weight. Circus performers, construction workers, and grocers all depend on the accurate measurement of weight in order to perform their tasks with ease and precision. In the 2D world of the screen, issues of balance are measured differently. Size, scale, value, and color, among other elements, create visual weight.

The balanced frame is equally weighted on both sides of the composition. Balance and an asymmetrical frame are not mutually exclusive. A distribution of differently scaled objects, contrasts in value, or even variations in color can create an asymmetrical composition. The element of balance is something that can be sensed, if not measured. It creates a world in which the eye travels unimpeded around and through the various forms it encounters.

IMBALANCE

Imagine a frame composed of a feather on one side and an elephant on the other. What does your eye travel to first, and where does it return? The imbalanced frame has a weight problem. This is not to say that there is something necessarily wrong with an imbalanced frame. The weight issue can always be worked to the advantage of the director or designer. If you are aware of the situation, you can utilize the composition to manipulate your audience's attention to a particular object or event. It is also an effective way to allude to the space outside the frame.

[*Potemkin,* 1925]

[*October,* 1928]

[*October,* 1928]

SERIES

Imagine a camera facing the side of a large office building. Rows of windows, all the same shape and size, fill the frame. The only variety comes from small, individual touches that are visible in each cubicle. This is a frame that is structured by a series.

A series is created by a repetition of form or line within the frame. The eye is met with a pattern that is repeated over and over. The viewer's attention will be immediately drawn to any element that is out of step in the established order.

RANDOMNESS

Randomness is more than an absence of order. It is an arrangement that alludes to a world that has not been touched by the manipulation of human hand or mind. This approach is deceptively difficult to achieve. In fact, it may take a great deal of planning to create a composition that looks random. Our minds demand order. Even when we attempt to create a less-than-orderly arrangement of objects, going against the mind's natural inclination to order is surprisingly difficult, and the "ordering" human hand can often still be seen or sensed in the design. Only skillful blocking that carefully mirrors chaotic movement will create a crowd scene that appears disorderly.

[*October,* 1928]

[*Alexander Nevsky,* 1938]

LINES AND SHAPES

A line is a vector, a connection of one point to another; it plots direction. Within the frame it can act as a powerful guide to lead the eye from one place of interest to the next. There are many examples of compositions that use linear strategies to structure the frame. Horizontal, vertical, and diagonal lines are among the most commonly used in film, video, and other two-dimensional projects.

[*Stagecoach,* 1939]

Film and video share a compositional similarity in that their formats are both limited to a rectangle that is horizontally oriented. The **horizontal line** is a reflection of the line that defines the width of the frame. Lines that mirror the horizon serve to underline the expanse of the rectangle. They can also create two or more rectangles within the frame. This compositional approach is often found in Westerns, where man's vertical stance is seen against the backdrop of an expansive horizon.

Vertical lines are reflections of the sides of the frame. They are found in shots or frames that feature a figure against a field, buildings against the sky, or any other element that reaches up in defiance of gravity.

[*Potemkin,* 1925]

The **diagonal line** splits the frame into triangles. It also serves to move the eye in a direction that leads outside the frame. This can be used to create dynamic motion from one shot to the next as well as movement within the single frame itself. The diagonal approach supports asymmetry and imbalance in the frame.

[*Potemkin*, 1925]

[*M*, 1931]

[*Gold Diggers of 1933*]   **CIRCLES**

[*M*, 1931]   **SQUARES**

[*Potemkin*, 1925]   **TRIANGLES**

CIRCLES, SQUARES, TRIANGLES, AND MORE

Sometimes a simple geometric shape serves every shot starts with the inescapable rectangle of the frame. The horizontal orientation is a given, no matter which aspect ratio is being utilized. What we sculpt inside that rectangle is another matter. In the three adjacent frames you can observe familiar shapes that offer strong, simple solutions to structuring the space inside the borders of a rectangular frame.

CONTRAST, TEXTURE, AND OTHER ELEMENTS OF THE IMAGE

There are also some subtler methods of manipulating the eye, aside from the obvious graphic structure of the frame. The texture of each form and the contrast between their values can express something about the world and the characters that inhabit the space and the time of the story. These elements are not as easily noticed by the audience but can contribute to the overall "read" of the picture.

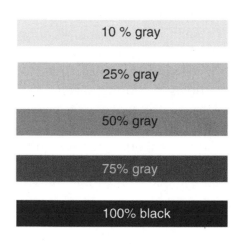

10 % gray

25% gray

50% gray

75% gray

100% black

CONTRAST

Contrast cannot exist without comparing one part of a frame to another. The type of contrast that this section refers to is one that is created by the juxtaposition of areas of different value. Value is the relative lightness or darkness of a color or a tone.

Contrast is often measured in terms of its percentage of relative darkness. Black is expressed as 100% and white as 0% so that a middle gray can be called a 45-55% value of gray. Values are not just used in black-and-white situations. Each color or hue has its own value translation, or relative lightness or darkness that can be expressed in terms of value.

The term "high contrast" refers to the use of a large spread of values within the frame, so that you will see both deep blacks and bright, sparkling whites within the same scene. A "low contrast" composition uses a limited spread of values, perhaps only 40% of the possible array of lights and darks.

The eye interprets darker values as receding in space and lighter ones as coming forward in the picture plane. Observe the frames to the left to see how your attention moves through the space in these examples of high and low contrast compositions.

TEXTURE

We tend to think of texture as something that is felt through the skin, an element of our sense of touch, not of sight. Although the world of images is flat, there are a variety of ways to add texture to a shot. The most all-encompassing is through the choice of different film stocks and lenses. It is beyond the scope of this volume to cover all the possibilities in this area, but a general understanding of grain and depth of field can be useful for anyone involved in creating images on film and video.

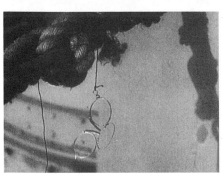

[*Potemkin,* 1925]

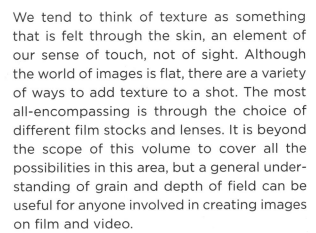

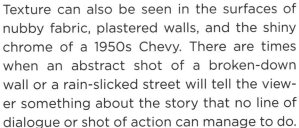

Texture can also be seen in the surfaces of nubby fabric, plastered walls, and the shiny chrome of a 1950s Chevy. There are times when an abstract shot of a broken-down wall or a rain-slicked street will tell the viewer something about the story that no line of dialogue or shot of action can manage to do.

[*Alexander Nevsky,* 1938]

This chapter has covered some of the most common strategies for structuring the frame. They are not mutually exclusive. Many frames use a combination of these elements and function beautifully in terms of aesthetics and narrative.

Of course, there are scripts that don't need such tightly composed shots. The liberal use of handheld shooting, as seen in John Cassavetes' *A Woman Under the Influence* (1974), Woody Allen's *Husbands and Wives* (1992), Lars von Trier's *Breaking the Waves* (1996), and in innumerable films shot in the "cinema verité" style, precludes the necessity of heavy preproduction visualization. In fact, to do so would be counter productive to telling those particular stories.

The script usually leads the way, but story can be subsumed by style. In other words, there is a delicate balance between the form of the composition and the content of the story. Use these tools with precision, but not necessarily in every frame or circumstance. Each decision carries the weight of the history of making pictures — perhaps a daunting challenge, but one that can also inspire new ways of seeing and telling great stories.

COMPOSITION EXERCISES:
GRID THE SCREEN AND PAINT THE FRAME

> Choose a film that you admire, but have not had a great deal of time to observe. (The film can be in color or black and white, but I recommend starting with a film that is black and white; with a gray scale image there are fewer elements to contend with, and fewer materials to assemble.)

> Stretch a piece of clear acetate over the screen of your television or monitor and secure it with tape on all sides. Then, with a chisel tip black marker, draw two diagonal lines that extend to each corner of the film frame. Where these cross in the center, draw vertical and horizontal lines that bisect the screen. (Remember that if you are watching a film that is being presented in a letterbox format, you need to draw the diagonals to that proportion, not to the corners of the screen.)

> Watch the film and observe the composition of each shot with reference to the lines on the screen. (It helps to have the volume on low.)

> Make note of the shots that interest you in terms of their visual structure. Then take three pieces of illustration board that have been cut to the aspect ratio of your film. I recommend using 9″ by 16.5″ for the 1.85 ratio or the equivalent for other ratios. Paint gray scale interpretations of the compositions of your chosen shots. You don't need to slavishly try to copy the frames. Allow yourself some creative freedom and have fun.

EXAMPLE OF GRIDDED SCREEN

[*Potemkin,* 1925]

DIRECTOR AT BLUE SKY STUDIOS

Art Director: *Robots*; **Director:** *Horton Hears a Who*

On Training

"I *always* knew I wanted to be involved with image creation. Part way through my education I took an introduction to animation class and did a little walking animation. When it was shown in class and people clapped, I felt an excitement that just went way beyond what I was experiencing in my graphic work. My first job after undergrad was with a company that did big multi-image slide shows for industrial clients. This was in the early '80s, and we also were doing some experimental light shows at night. Then I was lucky to get involved in one of the first graduate departments in computer graphics research, at Ohio State where I worked on computer-generated animation.

Back in '82–'83 we were still a good way off from doing interesting character animation, but because I was a designer out of that program and there was a production company on campus, I began doing their storyboard and concept design. So as I was going through school, I was also working in their design department and was able to work on real productions from the get-go — it was mostly sports and news graphics, flying logos and the like — but it was the newest thing, a really exciting time to be around. Actually, there was far more computing power at the company than at the university.

On Process

When we were doing commercials and broadcast design, the advertising agencies would give us simple concept boards. Then we'd re-board the commercial, working out specific camera staging, making it a real story. Once that was complete, you'd get back in there and pitch. The way we put our boards together communicated how we understood their challenges and offered interesting solutions as well.

Regarding animatics, there were times that we'd cut these images together, but often the turnaround on these commercial projects was so fast that literally you'd get a call and you'd be expected to have the presentation within a couple of days. If the job was ordered we then were in partnership with the agency, and so we'd have time to take the concept boards and throw in a temp track with a v.o. (voice over) and begin the process — kind of like preproduction.

In animation nowadays we cut the film first in pen and paper. The film is generated with story pads — we generate as many ideas as we can before we create any final animation. With computer animation you try to avoid any waste. The cost of this process means that you can't afford to produce the

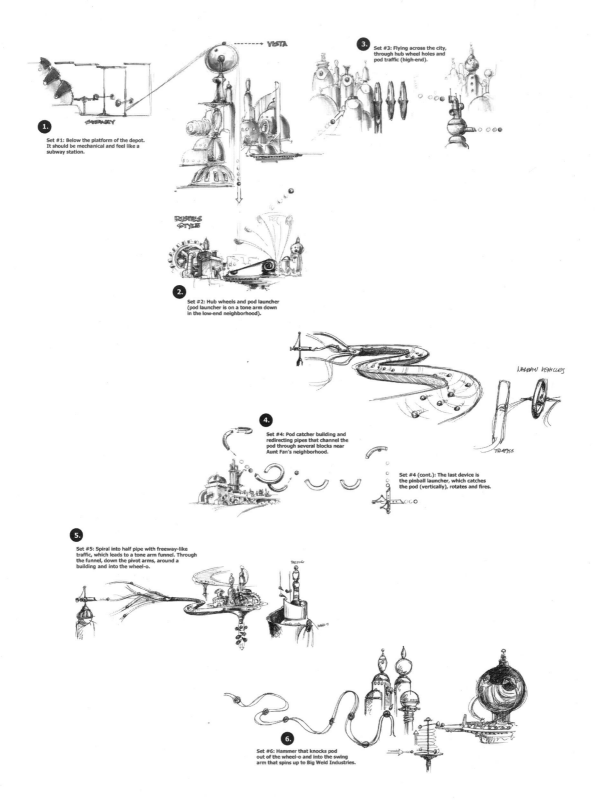

Set #1: Below the platform of the depot. It should be mechanical and feel like a subway station.

Set #2: Hub wheels and pod launcher (pod launcher is on a tone arm down in the low-end neighborhood).

Set #3: Flying across the city, through hub wheel holes and pod traffic (high-end).

Set #4: Pod catcher building and redirecting pipes that channel the pod through several blocks near Aunt Fan's neighborhood.

Set #4 (cont.): The last device is the pinball launcher, which catches the pod (vertically), rotates and fires.

Set #5: Spiral into half pipe with freeway-like traffic, which leads to a tone arm funnel. Through the funnel, down the pivot arms, around a building and into the wheel-o.

Set #6: Hammer that knocks pod out of the wheel-o and into the swing arm that spins up to Big Weld Industries.

amount of footage you have on live action. Similar to commercial production — you need a strong plan and know what part of the set you are going to see, how long the shots will be.

I find in feature animation what you build in terms of settings depends on the structure of the story. In *Horton Hears a Who* there's a big part of the story that's a journey. When you're a character on a journey, you move through space. So we looked at the kinds of shots that we needed to create this voyage, but didn't build all the sets in 360 degrees. We carefully chose the shots and just built the backgrounds that were needed. But in Whoville we knew we'd be there for many sequences, so we built that set completely.

On Art Direction

On *Robots* we used a different strategy. We'd build the sets about 75%, then as we'd shoot we'd add that last 25% of polish — more props, more modeling details. Once we locked in the specific shot sequences, we'd go in and set dress those last details. Quite a lot like live action, except that everything on set we had to create rather than go to the prop truck!

Art direction in animation is a much broader job description than in live action. As the art director, you're responsible for the imagery, the look of the movie. Not the characters' performances, but pretty much every other department. So on *Robots* I spent my days traveling to every other department to understand what the director was going for and bring the look and feel of the film together. When I first came on the project, I created a style guide for the look of the movie. We came up with a logic for what things looked like in Robot City. Putting that together became a guide for everyone working on the movie.

So I was responsible for helping to shape the director's vision for the film: the design of the sets, the props, the lighting. We'd also do a color script for the entire film; color keys and lighting guides for every sequence even setting the details for the lighting scheme — where the fill lights would be, who'd get a little rim light to highlight them from the background. Actually, an animation art director functions something like a Director of Photography might on a live action feature.

If you love what you're doing every day and you're around people that feel the same way, that's tremendous. I have a group of talented people around me all the time — it makes me stay on my game. You see things that inspire you, and it makes your workday a whole lot nicer. We push one another and not in a bad way."

LOSING IT, BRIEFLY

There are times when the extremely demanding hours of production bring out less than admirable behavior. The trick is to recover with grace and keep moving ahead. I was working on a shoot that was long on both hours and creativity. This being a combination that I eagerly pursue, I was pleased to be on the set late one night when a strange situation developed. It was 2 a.m. and we'd been shooting for hours, trying to finish a large crowd scene set in a hotel lobby. We were preparing for a stunt where someone would crash through one of the hotel's plate glass windows. Extras were milling about the lobby, drinking coffee and chatting quietly while the crew set up the next shot. It was my turn to collect all the craft service Styrofoam cups from the cast and extras on the set.

I approached a group of people sitting on a bench that was in the middle of the shot and asked them to please hand over their cups. One person in the group was using his cup as an ashtray and he refused to hand it to me. O.K, it was late and everyone tired, bored, and hungry, but the cameras were now about to roll. I asked again and the guy took the cup and hid it behind his back. Foolishly, I took the bait and reached behind him to nab it. He then decided to give it to me, and proceeded to crush the cup, butts and all, against my head.

This kind of rough play tends to escalate quickly. I hauled back and slapped him on the face and was rewarded with a kick to my shin. The crowd drew back, anticipating a real battle. I stand barely 5'3" and have no martial arts training, so I started screaming for reinforcements. The producer heard my cry, and as he walked over, I demanded that the hooligan be removed from the set.

It was then that I was informed that I had just struck an actor. Not a major one, but a necessary one, nonetheless. Embarrassed but not ashamed, I retreated to the relative calm of an adjacent room that the art department was using as a storage area. I was telling my side of the story to the crew when the producer came in and informed us that the actor was now refusing to work until he received an apology. Still hot with the passion of the fight, I refused. I was reminded that in this circumstance we needed to 'defer to talent.' I suggested that if that were the case, the actor should get down on his knees to me.

I was pissed. I had been roughed up in the course of performing my onset duties and an apology was not forthcoming. But nothing was getting accomplished. We had a hundred extras waiting around, and it was near 3 in the morning. Time to get off it. OK, I told him, I'll handle it. I went back to the set and approached my grumbling opponent. He sneered at me as I knelt by his side. I don't remember exactly what I said, but a few minutes later we shook hands and he went back to work. People working under high pressure and on little sleep can exhibit strange behavior. Sometimes it becomes necessary to remind yourself that it's only a movie.

> "There is no doubt that every color is a specific wavelength of energy that can represent or symbolize a life or time or emotion... visually movies are the resolution of a conflict between light and shadows. Light reveals truth and shadows obscure it, with a broad base of tonality in between."
>
> —Vittorio Storaro

INTRODUCTION

Imagine this scene: A high, wide shot of a spacious back yard circa 1950 — white chairs lined up facing a flowered arbor. Men in dark suits and tuxedos, ladies in pastel cocktail dresses are seated as we hear a wedding march begin to play. Cut to ground level looking back at the house and we see the bride emerge through French doors — wearing a knee-length, blood-red gown. Cut to the assembled crowd's reaction — darting glances, hidden smiles, distressed relatives.

What does this colorful design choice suggest to us? About her character, about the circumstances of the upcoming marriage, about the social norms of the period? Color has enormous significance in the reading of visual narrative and a basic understanding of some approaches to this issue can help to focus your visual thinking on story as well as execution.

WHY INVESTIGATE THE USE OF COLOR IN A BOOK ABOUT STORYBOARDING?

While many storyboards continue to be drawn in black and white, there are times when these editorial boards or key frames are also developed with color details. This process gives the director, DP, and designers an opportunity to have a conversation about the "color story" and coordinate their efforts in non-verbal narrative. The color story is embedded in the timeline of the film and can be seen in the progression of changes in hue, saturation, and relative brightness that is reflected in the characters and environments. As the film shifts from Act One information, such as the introduction of characters' background and goals, to Act Two complexities, including rising conflicts, there may be a change in pace as well as mood. These changes can be signaled with a shift of color palettes that relate to the new circumstances.

This chapter will investigate the areas of nature and culture that affect the way we read color. Examples from film as well as science, ethnography, and other allied fields will be examined in an attempt to understand this complex, fascinating, and often overlooked area of visual storytelling. The chapter will also offer a selection of field-tested exercises that will aid you in sharpening your color sensitivity and applying this knowledge to projects under development.

> **"I found I could say things with color and shapes that I couldn't say any other way — things I had no words for."**
>
> **— Georgia O'Keeffe**

UNDERSTANDING COLOR: AN EXPERIENTIAL GUIDE

Some researchers who study perception believe that the first color we are aware of is deep red — the shade that we sense through our closed eyelids in the womb. Once we open our eyes to the outer world it may take weeks, even months, for our eyes to adjust to the full spectrum of light. Once our sight is fully developed, we can perceive remarkably subtle differences in the greens of growing leaves and the blues of the oceans waters. Some evolutionary scientists believe that the development of this extraordinary sensitivity could have been responsible for early man's survival, enabling him to identify edible plants or hunting animals even when they presented only subtle differences of color and pattern from their surroundings.

Let's take a few moments to review some basic information about how and why we see color: Our eyes are complicated and sensitive instruments capable of sensing millions of variations of hue, value, and saturation. Small photoreceptors called cones are responsible for detecting these color variations and other receptors called rods are hard-wired for night vision, motion detection, and peripheral vision. Between these two we make our way through a three-dimensional world that holds a vast quantity of information in its visual display.

A SMIDGEON OF SCIENCE

The colors that we see are a function of our eyes' being able to perceive waves on the electromagnetic spectrum. The visible part of the spectrum reaches from violet on the short or high side to red on the long or low. Ultraviolet and infrared are just beyond our abilities to detect, but can be seen by other species such as birds and bees. The visible portion is just a small proportion of the electromagnetic spectrum, as you can see in the diagram below.

Human Perception

| Gamma Rays | X-rays | Ultraviolet | Visible | Infrared | Heat | Radio Waves |

USEFUL TERMS IN COLOR THEORY AND PRACTICE

HUE: the pure spectrum colors commonly referred to by the "color names" — red, orange, yellow, blue, green, or violet.

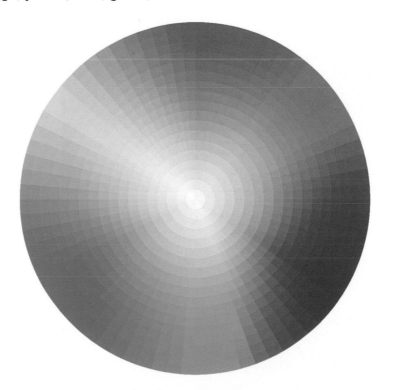

SATURATION (CHROMA): the purity of the hue. Fully saturated hues are pure of mixture with neutrals, black, or white. De-saturated colors have been diluted by the addition of white, black, neutral, or any other hue.

[*Do the Right Thing,* 1989]
Director: Spike Lee

SATURATED COLOR SYSTEM

[*Matewan,* 1987]
Director: John Sayles

DE-SATURATED COLOR SYSTEM

VALUE (INTENSITY): the relative lightness or darkness of a color. All hues have associated values, which are often expressed in a percentage, with 100% equaling black and 0%, white.

PRIMARY COLORS: the three colors by which all other hues can be mixed. There are different systems in use that vary from medium to medium.

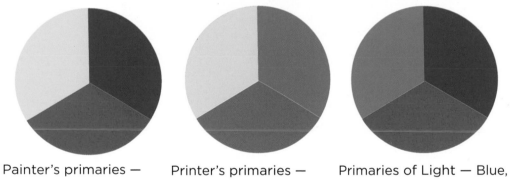

Painter's primaries — Red, Blue, and Yellow (subtractive)

Printer's primaries — Cyan, Yellow, Magenta (subtractive)

Primaries of Light — Blue, Red and Green (additive)

SECONDARY COLORS: The result of a mixture of 2 primaries

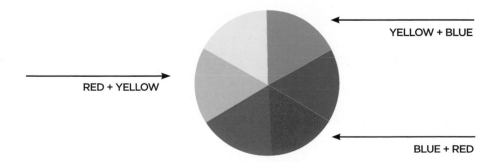

YELLOW + BLUE

RED + YELLOW

BLUE + RED

ADDITIVE COLOR: a method of mixing of two or more sources of light to create colors. White light is the result of mixing the three light primaries.

SUBTRACTIVE COLOR: a method of mixing pigment, whether of paint or ink. Mixing these primaries results in a dark gray/brown hue.

COMPLEMENTARY AND TRIADIC RELATIONSHIPS: Complementary colors are those hues that are found directly opposite each other (180 degrees apart) on the color wheel. Colors in triadic relationship are separated by 120 degrees on the color wheel. This frame from Jacques Demy's *Umbrellas of Cherbourg* demonstrates the use of complementary tints of green and red.

[*Umbrellas of Cherbourg*, 1964] Director: Jacques Demy

"WARM" COLORS: those in the yellow-orange-red range.

[*Far From Heaven* , 2002] Director: Todd Haynes

"COOL" COLORS: those in the blue-green-purple range.

[Far From Heaven, 2002]

ANALOGOUS COLORS: those that are adjacent on the color wheel. Think of color families such as red and orange.

[Umbrellas of Cherbourg, 1964]

CONTRAST: the relation between the perceived values of adjacent colors.

High Contrast

[*The Cook, The Thief,
His Wife, and
Her Lover,* 1989]
Director: Peter Greenaway

Low Contrast

[*Hero,* 2002]
Director: Yimou Zhang

SIMULTANEOUS CONTRAST: the relationship of two colors when adjacent and acting upon each other. Colors are rarely seen in isolation and our perception of each hue is affected by the surrounding environment.

[*Dodes Kade ,* 1970]
Director: Akira Kurosawa

MONOCHROMATIC COLOR: the use of a single dominant hue in a frame or project.

[*The Last Emperor,*
1987]
Director: Bernardo
Bertolucci

BICHROMATIC/TRICHROMATIC COLOR: the use of a two- or three-color strategy. The image from *Umbrellas of Cherbourg* is an example of a trichromatic frame.

[*Umbrellas of
Cherbourg,* 1964]
Director: Jacques Demy

EXERCISE 1:
APPLYING STRATEGIES TO STORYTELLING

Choose 3–5 of the preceding color strategies and create a storyboard/set of keyframes that use each of them in the context of visual storytelling.

The images can be drawn, photographed, or created with an imaging program.

Present the project to a group of colleagues and engage in a discussion regarding your use of color and how it might affect the reading of the story.

ANALOGOUS COLORS

MONOCHROME

SPLIT COMPLEMENTARY

EXERCISE 2:

Select a series of black and white images that have a narrative connection, as in stills from a film, or choose unrelated but visually compelling imagery from sources such as documentary photography or family snapshots. Scan the frames into an image processing program (such as Photoshop) and layer color onto the frames in a manner that reflects the color systems that have been discussed in this chapter. You can also treat a frame in more than one manner to gauge changes in emotional and narrative content.

This exercise can be very useful in deciding what palette to use in designing a film or other time-based media project. In that situation, using a selection of location photos and/or character images can help develop the conversation between director, designers, and cinematographer.

Student work by
Levan Tkabladze
Otis College of Art and Design

COLOR AND THE DEVELOPMENT OF STORY

Character by Way of Color

A film, or any other time-based narrative project that depends on visual media, takes place on a continuum. Perhaps we start out at a moment of initiation —a family has gathered for an inter-generational event (Coppola's *Godfather I*) or a ruler is about to pass on his inheritance (Kurosawa's *Ran*). Maybe a man has finished a long fight and has headed west to find a new life (*Dances with Wolves*) or a young man struggles with carving out his identity in a difficult family situation (*Rebel Without a Cause*). In each of these films, color plays a part in the audience's understanding of the main characters and their relationship to the world around them.

> "Mere color, unspoiled by meaning, and unallied with definite form, can speak to the soul in a thousand different ways."
>
> — Oscar Wilde

What do the muted colors of Don Corleone's study and the vibrant primary colors of the armies of *Ran* tell us about these extended families? In the case of *The Godfather* we see a family united, sharing the colors of the tribe assembled — black, white, some soft pastels, and subtle neutrals. Even friends of the family who have come to pay tribute and ask for favor dress in this accepted uniform.

[*The Godfather*, 1972]
Director: Frances Ford Coppola

When we look at *Ran*, though, the colors tell a very different story about the family that is at the heart of the film. The father dresses in white, a color that in the Japanese culture signifies wisdom and purity. But each of his children and their families have taken on a different, deeply saturated color. By the second act we see ties of this family come undone, as each faction squares off against each other on the battlefield and the contrasting colors of each sibling drape their armies.

[*Ran,* 1985]
Director: Akira
Kurosawa

In this way the color choices support the narrative structure of these scenes and help to set up the story arcs that will be constructed through the subsequent acts. Both scenes are examples of the use of family or tribal color signifiers to carry nonverbal information to the audience. Are most people conscious of this level of story structure? Probably not, but as creators it is another opportunity for us to communicate deeply and beyond words.

The character of Jim (James Dean) in Nicholas Ray's *Rebel Without a Cause* affords another example of the use of color to delineate character. This time it's the choice of a red leather jacket that sets the anti-hero apart from his suburban 1950s surroundings. To show that the family at the center of this film is culturally indistinguishable from its neighbors, the filmmakers dress and surround them in the same colors as the other members of this suburban setting. It is the wayward, rebellious son who wears a coat that sets him apart, not only from his family, but also from his classmates and the dominant culture of the time.

[*Rebel Without a Cause,* 1955] Director: Nicholas Ray

These three examples begin to delineate an approach to using color in an informed way that works to support the narrative. The next section will delve more deeply into different strategies that are used by motion media artists to go beyond written text as they seek to paint worlds with clarity as well as subtlety.

EXERCISE 3:
READING THE SCENE: BLACK AND WHITE TO COLOR

[*The Wizard of Oz*, 1939] Director: Victor Fleming

1. Working alone or in a small team, write and/or storyboard a scenario that can be expressed in 10-14 still images.
2. Shoot digitally and then create 2 sets of these images with one set having the color removed in Photoshop (or another image processing program).
3. Present the sequences: First show the black-and-white images, then the color versions. Finally lead a conversation about how the 2 sets of images led the viewer toward different ideas and experiences regarding the storyline. This discussion may serve to highlight various historical and cultural impressions that we carry about color and its narrative possibilities.

SPHERES OF COLOR:
STRATEGIES FOR APPLYING COLOR
TO STORY STRUCTURE

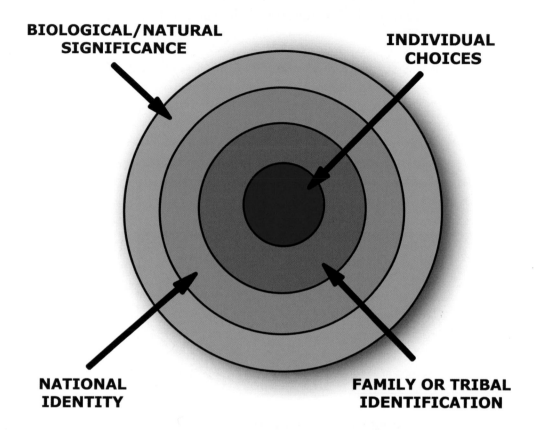

BIOLOGICAL/NATURAL SIGNIFICANCE

INDIVIDUAL CHOICES

NATIONAL IDENTITY

FAMILY OR TRIBAL IDENTIFICATION

Starting in the center, the rings of color grow as the number of people affected by the system grows. For instance, in the center, the color choices reflect/affect only a single individual. In the next circle, the reference is to families or tribes that might number in the tens or hundreds.

SPHERES OF COLOR — A SYSTEM TO ANALYZE AND PLOT COLOR USAGE

The preceding diagram lays out an approach to understanding different uses of color within a constructed world such as we find in film or animation. Starting from the center ring, it builds on the idea that as social units increase in size from the individual (smallest unit) through the biological (largest group), our interpretation of color usage shifts in reaction to these spheres of influence. The following examples will trace the use of these systems, starting with colors that are reflective of individual choices up through systems that are dependent on global and/or physiological experiences.

COLOR AND THE INDIVIDUAL (center ring)

The diagram's inner circle refers to a system of color that reflects an individual perspective. This approach locates color choices as springing from a unique psychological profile that may be influenced by the dominant culture or defined in opposition to it (see previous example from *Rebel Without a Cause* on page 153).

A variation of this strategy can be seen in Peter Greenaway's *The Cook, The Thief, His Wife, and Her Lover.* The use of color in this film is idiosyncratic to the degree that a character's clothing might change as she walks from room to room. The filmmaker, who has a practice as an artist as well as a film director, colors the film's three locations. By making the dining room, kitchen, and parking lot of a sumptuous restaurant correspond to the three primaries of light, he keys the emotional environments of the film's scenes to those colors.

[*The Cook, The Thief, His Wife, and Her Lover,* 1989] Director: Peter Greenaway

THE DINING ROOM

THE KITCHEN

[*The Cook, The Thief, His Wife, and Her Lover*, 1989]

THE PARKING LOT

A similar use of color can be seen in *Pleasantville*, directed by Gary Ross. In this film the characters inhabit a gray world, a stereotypical 1950s America lived as something out of black-and-white television. As the characters begin to act on their yearnings for a more authentic life, their world is transformed into a passionate, colorful landscape. But rather than simply switching from a palette of grays to one of color, the filmmakers have the deeply saturated hues bleed into the gray world; the bleeding not only adds color but acts as a metaphor for infusing their existence with life.

[*Pleasantville,* 1998]
Director: Gary Ross

Finally, Bernardo Bertolucci's *The Last Emperor* offers an excellent example of the use of color to describe an individual's psychic journey in nonverbal terms. Drawing from cinematographer Vittorio Storaro's deep investigation into the relationship between color and human experience, this film traces the life of Pu Yi, considered by many to be the final emperor of China. In Storaro's book *Writing With Light* (*Accademia dell'Immagine*, 2002), he outlines his concept of the "Ages of Color."

Positing a personal symbology of color, he details the progression as follows:

"BLACK   is the color of Conception
RED   Birth (blood)
ORANGE   Growth (warmth of family as a child)
YELLOW   Light, education
GRAY   Waiting (for the education to develop into knowledge, wisdom)
GREEN   Knowledge
BLUE,   Intelligence
INDIGO,   Consciousness
VIOLET,   Maturity
The sum of these colors is WHITE, the color of LIFE."

With these equivalences in mind, the creative team crafted a personal journey through the decades of Pu-Yi's life. This investigation adhered to the color palette as defined above, painting an evocative portrait that expressed narrative structure in color as well as action and dialogue.

[*The Last Emperor,* 1987]
Director: Bernardo
Bertolucci

WHITE — THE COLOR OF LIFE

YELLOW — THE COLOR OF LIGHT AND EDUCATION

GREEN — THE COLOR OF FREEDOM

COLOR AND FAMILY/TRIBE (second ring)

The tribe is the next largest social unit beyond the individual. This group can be seen as having an extended family structure and is often visually characterized by similarity of color associations. A strong example of this strategy can be found in films that have stories at their center that focus on family or tight community relationships.

West Side Story reflects a mid-twentieth-century example of this approach. As in many musical dramas, the colors are highly saturated, and it is easy

[*West Side Story,* 1961]
Director: Robert Wise

JETS IN YELLOWS AND BLUES AT THE DANCE.

SHARKS IN PURPLE AND ORANGE, COMPLEMENTARY COLORS TO THE JETS' YELLOW AND BLUE.

THE HOT SHARKS IN RED AND THE COOL JETS IN BLUE FACE OFF AT THE RUMBLE.

to differentiate at a glance between the worlds of the Sharks and the Jets. From the color to the form of their costumes, in the dance sequences as in the rumble, the two cultural worlds are differentiated by their distinctive palettes.

Another work to observe for the application of the idea of color signifying family or tribe is Kurosawa's *Ran*. Based loosely on Shakespeare's *King Lear*, this film follows the head of a powerful family in feudal Japan as he attempts to pass on his power to his children and their spouses. Internecine battles break out among the disparate groups and on the battlefield, color differentiates one family army from the next.

[*Ran,* 1985]
Director: Akira
Kurosawa

THE ARMIES DIVIDE AS THE KING EMERGES FROM A BLAZING CASTLE.

THE PRIMARY COLORS ARE ASSIGNED TO VARIOUS HEIRS TO THE THRONE.

Finally, another look at Todd Haynes' *Far From Heaven* reveals a striking correlation between members of the film's social circles (a modern interpretation of tribal structure) and the colors that they present to the world.

[*Far From Heaven*, 2002]
Director: Todd Haynes

CATHY (JULIANNE MOORE) HAS COFFEE WITH FRIENDS.

COLOR AND CULTURE: NATIONAL IDENTITY AND ITS PRESENTATION (third ring)

The third ring represents national allusions to color. In this schema the hues are used to define a wider boundary than the first two approaches. Narratives that deal with war and politics often utilize color in this manner. One set of films with palettes based on national colors was Krzysztof Kieslowski's *Trois Couleurs* series. Each film, both in content as well as form, was structured on the color and meaning of the French Flag, also known as the *tricolore*. The blue, white, and red colors of the flag are associated with the national motto: "liberty, equality, fraternity."

[*Blue*, 1993]
Director: Krzysztof
Kieslowski

[*White*, 1994]

[*Red*, 1994]

Color and Cultural Reference

In Zhang Yimou's *Hero*, Nameless is a local official who assassinates three of the ruling king's enemies. When he arrives at the king's home, he tells these stories with different emphases. The colors of both the settings and the character's dress change as the narration progresses through various versions of his narrative. In China the color red has connotations specific to that culture: In addition to standing for the nation, it is seen as the color of prosperity and happiness. The prevalent use of this color in one of the story sections relates to the development of China as a nation.

[*Hero,* 2002]
Director: Zhang Yimou

MOON AND FLYING SNOW DO BATTLE IN THE RED FOREST.

"Nora (Chavooshian, the production designer) and the director of photography Haskell Wexler, worked together on controlling the texture and color of what went in front of the camera, establishing a period look with design rather than filters or by treating the film stock...the bright contemporary edge was taken off by using a limited palette — blacks, browns, grays, grayish blues, and greens — almost no pure reds, or whites or yellows."

— John Sayles
Thinking in Pictures

COLOR AND NATURE (outer ring)

Nature is another source of palettes that can help create powerful associations in the viewer. Whether it is a collection of variegated greens in a landscape or the deep bluish-red of spilt blood, color choices pulled from nature can function as a visual reminder of our shared human experience.

John Sayles' *Matewan* offers a good example of this approach. It is a story about a coal mining town in West Virginia circa 1930. The townspeople are locked in battle with the company that runs the mine. The colors of nature — the brown of the earth, the blue of the sky, and the green of the hills — are reflected in the clothing of the locals. And the filmmakers assign a stark palette of black and white to the representatives of the coal mine and the church whose pastor supports them against the union organizers.

[*Matewan*, 1975]
Director: John Sayles

THE MINERS AND FAMILIES GATHER.

THE COMPANY MEN SCHEME.

Another example of a film that contrasts the colors of nature against those of culture is Werner Herzog's *Fitzcarraldo*, which follows an opera-obsessed German played by Klaus Kinski in his quest to build an opera house in the Amazon jungle. Fitzcarraldo's white suit contrasts with the palette of the jungle and its Indian inhabitants. We see a man pitted against nature as he attempts to drag a large river boat over an inconveniently placed mountain.

[*Fitzcarraldo,* 1982] Director: Werner Herzog

FITZCARRALDO, DRESSED IN AN INCONGRUOUS WHITE SUIT

NOTE THAT THE INDIGENOUS PEOPLE ARE ALL DRESSED IN THE COLOR OF THE EARTH

Additional examples can be found in various films where natural surroundings serve almost as characters themselves. In such an instance, the setting may function as an antagonist or an obstacle to the protagonist's goal.

> "In no reliable sense can we speak of color 'as it really is'; it is always determined by its context."
>
> —Rudolph Arnheim

EXERCISE 4
COLOR MOOD BOARDS FOR CHARACTER AND ENVIRONMENT

Mood boards are an excellent way to explore a character or a setting's colors, as well as their textures and patterns, outside the requirements of naturalism. Mood boards often take the form of collages and can be developed both in digital or analogue form. They can help the director, cinematographer, and design team coordinate efforts and be a starting point for spirited conversation regarding the development of the visual story.

EXERCISE A: OBSERVATION — Select a film that intrigues you in terms of its color use. Look at the structure of the entire film and identify act breaks. Choose 3 scenes from each act to observe and make notes on the use of color (as well as texture, shape, and pattern, if you like). Then take these notes and create one image for each act that expresses the use of these visual elements. Feel free to use abstract as well as representational imagery in the construction of these images. Be aware of any shifting in hue, value, saturation, and texture from act to act. If using this exercise in a classroom setting, try presenting your work without text (or film title) and asking for feedback from the group.

EXERCISE B: APPLICATION — Similar in format to the Observation version of this exercise, but shifts from looking out at other's work to looking inside and conceptualizing your own. Take a script and note the act breaks. If you have not yet created a book of visual reference, this is an excellent opportunity to do so. You can chose from photos, ads, images of paintings, scraps of fabric, even found objects. This exercise is as much about intuition as it is about exposition. Once you have assembled a rich selection of source material, begin to sort it into piles that begin to express your ideas about characters, settings, and events.

Be loose, be creative — a mood board is about a collection of ideas, not "correct decisions." Allow yourself to play and be abstract in your choices and materials. You can also explore a motion-graphic version of the mood board. Scan in images, set them to motion in iMovie (or any other editing program), and lay in some music.

Looking for examples and inspiration? Try Google images, "Mood Boards," where you'll find current examples of boards for film, fashion, graphic design and interiors.

> "Color is part of the language we speak with film. We use colors to articulate different feelings and moods. It is just like using light and darkness to symbolize the conflict between life and death. I believe the meanings of different colors are universal, but people in different cultures can interpret them in different ways."
>
> — Vittorio Storaro
> *American*
> *Cinematographer,* 1998

COLOR STRATEGIES

Design decisions, often made during pre-production and developed with the use of mood boards and concept sketches, carry significant weight in storytelling as they utilize the *visual structure of images*. These structures contain information that, although not overtly stated in dialogue, can nonetheless speak to audiences through emotional and cultural signifiers. Such structures contain information that allows for multiple readings and can relay various levels of the story through several different methodologies including:

> Juxtaposition
> Direct Reference
> Inference

Juxtaposition is a strategy that takes advantage of two systems used for contrast. The example from *Rebel Without a Cause* mentioned earlier can be interpreted in this manner, as we see the color choice of the individual (Jim Stark's red jacket) played off against the suburban palette of pastels (Natalie Wood's Judy in pink) and neutrals (Jim Backus' Frank Stark and Sal Mineo's Plato in black, browns, and whites).

Direct reference is used to strong effect in the *Wizard of Oz*, one of the first color Hollywood mega-musicals. The bad witch is dressed in black, the good one in white, and that yellow brick road can be seen as a stand-in for the dream of a path to opportunity paved in gold. The color scheme in this film is a straightforward interpretation of Western color signifiers. In other words, these choices have been made to coincide with our culture's most obvious interpretation.

Inference has to do with implication — a meaning is implied rather than stated outright. This approach springs from more subtle relationships in the reading of color. Just as in literature, a word or phrase can sometimes supply a direct meaning, while in other contexts it can also refer to its opposite. "What a memorable day" has one meaning when spoken by a traveler standing atop a Tuscan hill in April but quite another when muttered by a journalist reporting from a hill in an African war zone. In other words, the context creates meaning. A good example of this can be found in Bertolucci's *The Last Emperor* where he and his cinematographer, Vittorio Storaro, created a world of color meanings that were specific to that film. (See page 158 for more on this example.)

Now, for many of us in the creative fields of storytelling, these ingrained relationships may represent a first set of choices. But there are certainly other possibilities that exist within the varied spheres of color influence, as other cultures as well as domains of knowledge are investigated.

A very useful book in understanding the plentitude of relationships of color to meaning is to be found in *The Primary Colors* by Alexander Theroux (1994). Mr. Theroux has made an exhaustive study of the use of color in a great variety of disciplines, including but not limited to biology, anthropology, literature, fine art, and political systems. Here are a few examples:

Calling RED the boldest of colors, Theroux writes, "It stands for charity and martyrdom, hell, love, youth, fervor, boasting, sin, and atonement....[BLUE] is the symbol of baby boys in America, mourning in Borneo, tribulation to the American Indian, and the direction South in Tibet. Blue indicates mercy in the Cabala, and carbon monoxide in gas canisters."

YELLOW is connected positively with the color of butter, sponges, tennis balls, candlelight, pencils, rain slickers and McDonald's golden arches. But on a darker note, says Theroux, "It is the color of early bruises, unpopular cats, potato wart, old paper, chloroflavedo in plants, forbidding skies, dead leaves, xanthoderma, purulent conjunctivitis, dental plaque, gimp lace, foul curtains, infection, and pus ('yellow matter custard, dripping from a dead dog's eye,' sings John Lennon in 'I Am the Walrus'), speed bumps, callused feet, and ugly deposits of nicotine on fingers and teeth."

Color and pattern can work in similar ways. Imagine the reporter from our earlier example wearing her dusty khaki fatigues while in the battlefield. Then transplant the image of her in that attire to a child's birthday party or an afternoon wedding, and the "reading" of that color (among other things) will certainly change. These examples may seem a bit obvious, but the point is that *context is all* in this method of nonverbal messaging.

EXERCISE 5
USING COLOR AND IMAGERY AS AN AID TO WRITING

Try out this exercise in observation: Sit in an area where you can watch people you don't know well. A busy cafeteria, a bus stop, a sports event all work well. Choose someone in the crowd and look carefully at how they are presenting themselves. What color are their shoes — and are they polished or scuffed? Are they wearing a uniform that allows them to blend into the crowd or are they dressed to stand out? Now write for 10 minutes about this person. It may be a character sketch or a monologue that you imagine they will say to some-one they meet later in the day. Use all the visual cues in their appearance to inspire your writing. And in your descriptions, be sure to use the colors these people have chosen to surround themselves with in support of the story you are crafting.

AN ENDING AND A BEGINNING

This chapter has explored an introductory conversation regarding the use of color in the structure of story. As you consider the design of any project that involves pictorial as well as spoken or written storytelling elements, it may serve you to simply observe a scene quietly and see what is being communicated beyond words. In simply becoming aware of these distinctions, your creative process will deepen and your ability to communicate will include fluency in this subtle and expansive nonverbal language.

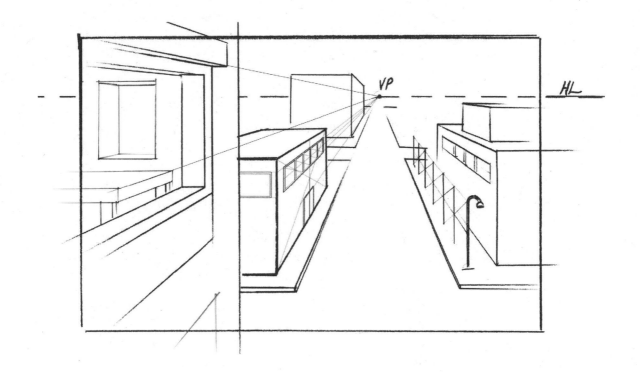

AN INTRODUCTION TO PERSPECTIVE

Perspective: from the Latin "prospectus," *to look forward*

WHY PERSPECTIVE?

Perspective is a topic that rarely surfaces when talking about film, but it is crucial to any discussion about translating the three-dimensional world into the two-dimensional plane of the film frame.

The world that surrounds us is one of three dimensions. The room you are sitting in is defined by width, length, and height. A piece of paper or strip of film

> "...any person of sound mind can learn to draw; the probability is the same for learning to read."
>
> —Betty Edwards
> *Drawing on the Artist Within*

has only two dimensions that are used for the image that rests upon it. In order to refer to the three dimensions of space on a two-dimensional surface, we need a drawing convention, an illusion that will trick the eye into thinking that the flat image has depth. Western art has developed a system of technical perspective that is invaluable to creating accurate storyboards; this chapter will spend some time helping you to become familiar with this drawing system.

In perspective, the parallel lines that define an image's depth converge to a spot called the vanishing point. In this chapter you will learn how to place your camera position to correspond with your vanishing points, so your sketch will accurately reflect your intended shot. There is perhaps no better way to immediately improve your ability to communicate about the visual world than to learn this method of representation.

The prospect of learning this new material may seem daunting to some of you. I can only tell you that I have seen remarkable progress in just a few hours from students who walk into classes and workshops with little or no previous drawing experience. The perspective drawing system in this book has been developed using the architectural approach as a starting point, but has been substantially simplified for the benefit of filmmakers and professionals in related fields.

HOW WE LEARN: A DIAGRAM

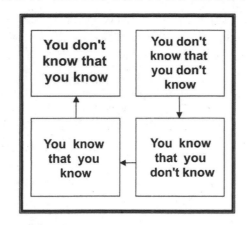

EXAMPLE OF STUDENT PROGRESS

BEFORE

AFTER

BEFORE

AFTER

Upper images: Nick Hill
Lower images: Michael Bertucci

PERSPECTIVE IN YOUR ENVIRONMENT

The room you are sitting in is most likely constructed from walls that are at 90-degree angles to each other. If you're sitting at a table, the same is probably true for the relationship of its top and legs. Many, if not most, of the man-made objects in our environment are built on the right angle. It is easy to join together and creates strength in both lateral and vertical directions.

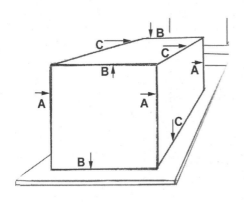

A = VERTICAL LINES
B = HORIZONTAL LINES
C = NEEDS VANISHING POINT!

In a cube we have three sets of facets, which correspond to the height, depth, and length of three-dimensional space. When one or more of these facets are parallel to one side of our picture plane, then only the remaining sides will require vanishing points for the lines that define them in pictorial space. Perspective drawing is based on the relationship of the sets of parallel faces that result in objects built on right angles.

When looking at a cube straight-on, the top of the cube is parallel to the top edge of your imaginary picture plane. The sides of the cube are parallel to the vertical edges. Only the planes that describe the depth of the cube are not in a parallel relationship with your picture plane. Those are the edges that need a vanishing point to describe the illusion of depth in the frame.

If we now rotate that cube so that the front plane is on a 45-degree angle to the picture plane, then that plane as well as the previous plane needs vanishing points.

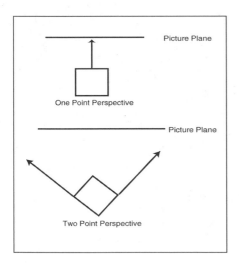

PERSPECTIVE

VOCABULARY

Station point: The position of the observer. The placement of the camera. This position can be plotted in the overhead diagram.

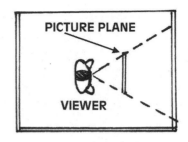

Picture plane: An imaginary plane set at a 90-degree angle to the observer, onto which the image of the scene is projected.

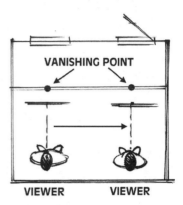

Imagine that you are holding a rectangular sheet of Plexiglas straight out in front of your body, and you are gazing through it at the world. That rectangle is acting as the picture plane. It is the two-dimensional surface that acts as projection screen for the three-dimensional world.

Horizon line: An imaginary line that is determined by the height of the camera or the observer of a scene.

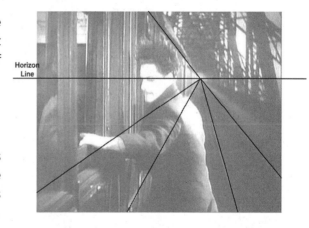

Vanishing point: A point that lies on the horizon and acts as a guide for the plotting of lines and planes that describe depth in the drawing.

Plan view (schematic): The layout of a scene from overhead. This is a diagram, not a drawing, of an overhead view of the set. Often used to situate camera positions within the sets. The plan view, or schematic, is used in perspective to plot the station point (camera position) in relation to the set pieces that are to be rendered.

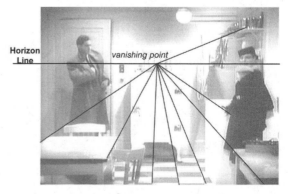

Cone of vision (field of view): The perimeter of the observer's vision. In film, the cone of vision, also called "field of view," is limited by the aspect ratio of the frame. This field of view shifts according to the length of the lens used for the shot. The longer the lens, the narrower the cone of vision.

One-point perspective: The situation of needing only one vanishing point to describe depth in a scene. When we are looking at a cube straight on, the top and the bottom planes of that cube will be parallel to the top and the bottom of the picture plane. The sides of the cube will be parallel to the vertical edges of the picture plane. Those planes will be described by lines that are horizontal and vertical. Only the planes that give the cube its depth will need to be described by lines that converge. These lines will converge at the vanishing point.

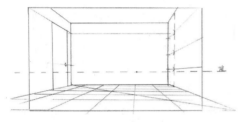

ONE-POINT = FRONTAL SHOTS, STRAIGHT-ON DOWN STREET OR DIRECTLY TO WALL OF ROOM

WHEN TO USE ONE-POINT PERSPECTIVE

This system of perspective is used for sketching shots that are seen from frontal angles. The camera is placed straight-on to the back wall in interior shots and looks straight onto a building or down the street in exterior shots.

Two-point perspective: This is used in situations when two vanishing points are needed to communicate depth — as when the cube is placed at an angle to the observer and the only set of planes that is parallel to the picture plane are the vertical ones. In this orientation, both sides of the cube are angled away from the observer and each set of lines that describe those sides will need its own vanishing point.

WHEN TO USE TWO-POINT PERSPECTIVE

When you are setting up an interior shot that looks into a room corner or is at a raking angle (a position that is not square) in relation to the walls of the room, you will be using a two-point setup. Each wall will need its own vanishing point, as they are both carving the depth of the room space.

In exterior scenes, a camera that is viewing a building or street scene from a 3/4 angle will create a need for two vanishing points in your drawing.

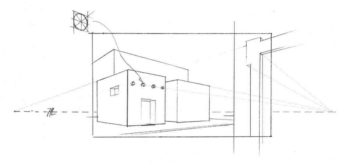

Three-point perspective: A system used when the object has no faces that are parallel to the picture plane. The vertical lines as well as the lines parallel to the floor are drawn to vanishing points.

WHEN TO USE THREE-POINT PERSPECTIVE

Usually for very high or low shots, when you need to convey the height of an object or building that is receding into the distance.

**TWO-POINT =
3/4-ANGLE SHOTS,
RAKING ANGLES,
OBLIQUE ANGLES**

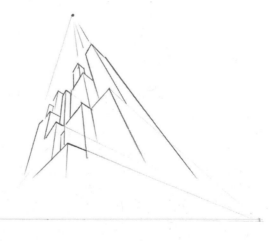

**THREE-POINT =
HELICOPTER SHOTS,
WORM'S EYE VIEW**

THE PENCIL HITS THE PAPER

The next section will cover the use of the perspective system in sketching storyboard imagery. It will cover both one- and two-point perspective systems and their application in creating a sketch that takes into account the camera height and position relative to the set and characters.

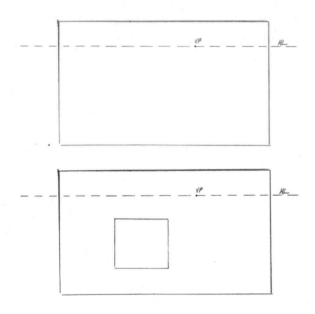

Drawing a Cube in One-Point Perspective

Start by making a frame on your paper. Using a 6" by 10-1/2" frame will give you an approximation of the 1.85 aspect ratio that is used as a standard in American projection projects. After completing your frame, select a camera height by placing your horizon line some distance between the top and bottom edge of the frame. Start with selecting a high camera and draw a light line 1/4 of the way down from the top of the frame. The horizon line will be a horizontal line, unless the shot is set at a canted angle.

Once the horizon line is set, choose a position for the vanishing point. In one-point perspective, the vanishing point will always be on the horizon, equidistant from the sides of the frame.

Next, draw the front face of the box as a regular square. Remember that any face of the cube that is parallel to the top and the bottom of the frame can be drawn with vertical and horizontal lines. Only the faces that describe the depth of the cube will need a vanishing point as a guide.

Now that you have the front face of the cube, use the vanishing point to determine the angle of the sides and the top face of the cube. Use the vanishing point as a pivot and draw light lines from the corners of the front face back towards the horizon. These lines are "imaginary" and by drawing them to the horizon they have an infinite distance.

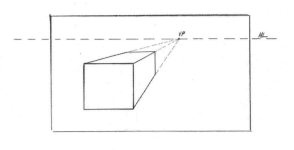

To finish off the cube, pass a vertical line through the bottom and the middle lines that you have just drawn. Where that line touches the top of the box, draw a horizontal line over to describe the back edge of your cube.

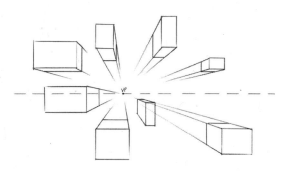

Transforming the Box into an Exterior Street Scene

Once you have drawn this cube in perspective, begin to expand the drawing into a high-angle street scene. The box can be easily made into a building by adding doors, windows, and other architectural details.

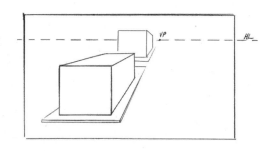

Any doors or windows that appear on a front face (a regular rectangle) will be drawn with vertical and horizontal lines. Any details added to the planes that have been drawn using the vanishing points will also use those points to determine the angles of their upper and lower edges.

Adding streets is easy. Imagine that they are flat planes, like the bottoms of unfinished cubes, which create a grid around your cube-buildings. By using horizontal lines to send the streets across the frame and lines that aim toward the vanishing point to send the streets back into the depth of the drawing, you can create a scene that has a look of solid reality about it.

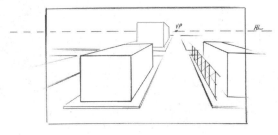

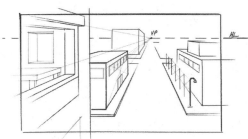

When you want to give those streets a curb, use a vertical line to drop down a small distance and then draw two more lines, one across the frame and another into the depth by way of the vanishing point.

Now have some fun. Add in buildings across the street, further back in the scene, and behind the ones in the foreground. Add a row of trees or telephone poles that diminish in height as they approach the vanishing point. Draw a box in above the horizon line and see what happens.

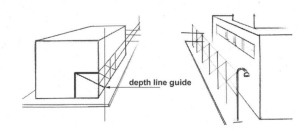

depth line guide

Measuring Depth in One-Point Perspective Space

You can measure the depth of your object by the "eyeball" method and approximate the back edge by taking into consideration the decreasing size of the object's face as it recedes in space. Or, there is a method that allows you to use diagonal lines as guides to measure equal distances into the distance.

Begin by bisecting a vertical line of your box with a small mark. Pass a line from the opposite corner of the cube through that mark, and continue on until it crosses the bottom edge of a side. Where the two lines intersect, draw a vertical line, and you will have drawn a box that is equal in measurement across the front and the sides.

ONE-POINT PERSPECTIVE INTERIORS

Now that you have the tools to draw boxes from the outside, let's go inside the box and draw the interior of a bedroom set.

Draw a frame as you did at the beginning of the last drawing. The first decision to make on the interior plan is

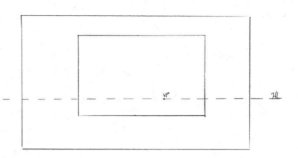

to decide how much of the back wall is visible in the shot. If you are shooting down a long corridor, the back wall might appear as a small, vertically-oriented rectangle. If we are in a ballroom, then the back wall might be represented as a long, horizontal rectangle.

Since the camera's height will determine the height of the horizon line, the back wall must be drawn in before the horizon line is set. Choose a height for your camera and draw in the horizon as a horizontal line crossing through the back wall.

If the horizon line is drawn in above the back wall, that would signify a camera that is above the height of the set walls. There are some circumstances where this would be appropriate, but most situations call for the camera to be inside the room.

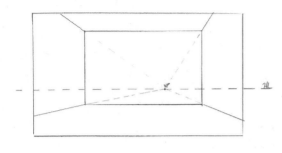

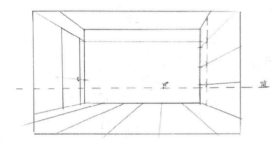

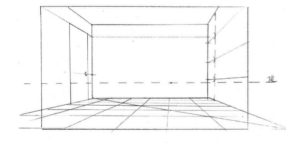

The rear wall of the room does not need to be centered in the frame. The camera can be closer to either sidewall, if desired, but in any case the vanishing point will be centered in the frame.

Mark the vanishing point on the horizon line and draw the lines that will delineate your walls, floor, and ceiling, passing each line through a corner of the rear wall and using the vanishing point as a guide to its angle.

Once the walls are set, then begin to add the details of the room: a door, a couple of windows, and perhaps a floor rug. Remember as you move around the room that any detail appearing on a wall that is drawn as a rectangle will also appear as a rectangle. Any detail appearing on a wall that is drawn to the vanishing point will also use the vanishing point to determine its top and bottom edges.

ADDING FURNITURE TO THE INTERIOR SCENE

Just as the truck in the exterior scene was carved out of a box, the same method can be used to create furniture for the bedroom (or any other interior scene). To begin, locate the position of the bed by drawing a rectangle on the floor, the "footprint" of the object. To work in scale, we can apply the technique that we used in the previous example to work out the measurement of the sidewalls.

Mark out equal divisions on the horizontal floor line. Then use the vanishing point to extend them with light lines into the room.

Draw a square in the corner of the back wall and bisect the side of the square that lies on the floor. Then pass a line through that mark from the vanishing point and out into the floor space. Where that line crosses each light line, you can draw a horizontal. Notice that the space between those lines increases as you move farther out into the room. Although that is the case, the lines represent equal distances along the floor. You can use this technique to scale the objects that you place in the room.

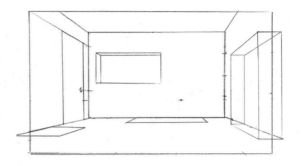

Once the bed's footprint is in place, raise one corner of it using a vertical line. Use the height of your back wall as a measure to make sure that the bed is in scale with the rest of the room. Once the height is set, then complete the cube. Make it into a bed by adding boxes on top with rounded edges that will become pillows and softening the lines of the large box to give it the visual feel of a mattress and bedding.

CHAIRS, BOOKCASES, ETC.

A slightly more complex form is the upholstered chair. Again, start with a footprint to give you the location of the chair in the room. Draw the facing plane first using vertical and horizontal lines. Then use the vanishing point to extend those lines to the back of the cube. As you do this, think of carving the space of the box. Look over the following examples of familiar furniture shapes that can be carved from cubes.

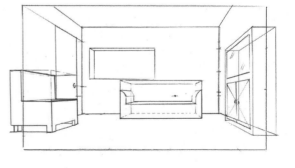

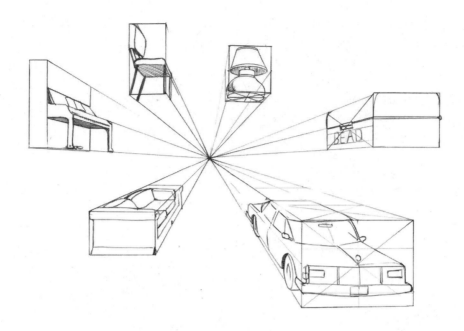

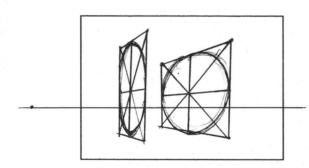

CIRCLES IN PERSPECTIVE

Let's say that you have a hanging, cylindrical lamp on your set. Unless you are looking straight at the underside of the cylinder, the circle will appear as an ellipse when you draw it in perspective. In order to find the correct shape for the circular edge, first construct a square in perspective at the level of the lampshade. Then connect the opposite corners with straight lines. This will give you the center of your ellipse. Using the midpoint, draw two lines that bisect the rectangle and are either parallel to the edges or vanishing to the horizon. These four lines will touch the polygon at eight points. Now use these points as a guide to drawing the ellipse.

TWO-POINT PERSPECTIVE

The next point of view is that of looking into a corner of a room or at a building at a 3/4 angle. In this situation, you need two vanishing points for the two sets of planes that describe the depth of the space. First, we will set up a high, wide shot of a city street.

Draw a frame as you did in the last exercise. A 9″ by 16″ rectangle will give you a frame with an aspect ratio that approximates the American projection standard of 1.85. The horizon line will signify the height of the camera, so draw a horizontal line passing through the upper third and extending out to the sides of the frame. That is the line that the vanishing points will be drawn on.

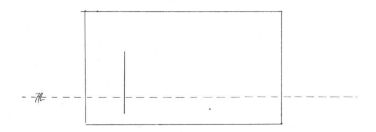

Here's where the simple sketch method is different from the architecturally precise one. In an architectural perspective draw-ing, an artist will draw out the setting on a plan view or overhead drawing. Then each point on this overhead is carried out to the picture plane, drawn up into an elevation, and then finally taken back to the vanish-ing points in order to finish the perspective sketch. This is a time-consuming, if visually precise, way of rendering the scene.

We are going to skip a few steps. This will require you to take a few matters on trust, but the ends should justify these reduced means.

HOW TO FIND THE VANISHING POINTS IN TWO-POINT PERSPECTIVE

The distance between the two vanishing points is determined by the length of the camera's lens and its distance from the subject. Changing lenses is tantamount to changing the observer's distance from what he or she is looking at as well. As the lens length changes — i.e., gets wider — the picture plane moves further away from the subject of the shot. As this happens the vanishing points spread out further and further. If the lens length grows longer, then the picture plane moves in.

If we dispense with the steps of drawing an overhead and plotting the points of the set onto an elevation, then we need a quick way of determining the placement of the vanishing points by eye. The suggested placement is one-half a frame's distance outside the frame on either side for a natural, 50mm lens length appearance.

1/2 width of frame

VP   VP

You will find that if you decrease this space and place the points next to the frame, you will end up with a drawing in which the objects begin to show distortion as they near the vanishing points. This distortion would be similar to what you would find if you were shooting with an 18mm lens.

The distance between the two vanishing points is relative to the distance of the picture plane from the object. The points can be equidistant from the frame, which describes an object that is angled 45 degrees to the picture plane.

When the angle of the object changes, the vanishing points move along the horizon line so that one or the other is closer and the other is further away, keeping the same relative distance as they move.

The longer the lens, the farther out from the frame the vanishing points will appear.

DRAWING A BOX IN TWO-POINT PERSPECTIVE, EXTERIOR SCENE

After you draw a frame, choose a height for the camera. Lay in the horizon line, and for a natural-looking image, place the vanishing points approximately one half a frame's width outside the frame. This will keep the angles of the drawing from getting too severe, which can happen when the points are drawn too close to the frame. Think of the distortion that an 18mm lens can create when shooting objects close-up.

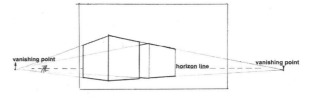

Once the vanishing points are in place, draw in a vertical line that will stand for the height of the box on the edge that is closest to the camera. Now use the vanishing points to draw in the sides and the top of the box. With this method, you will "eyeball" the distance to the back edge of the object.

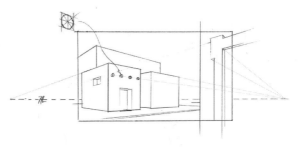

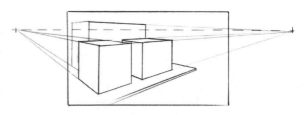

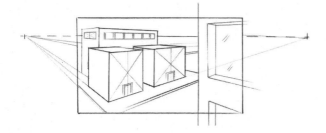

Once you have the two-point perspective cube drawn, enlarge the image so that you have another street scene. Try giving it some character, like an old-style street out of a Western or a futuristic scene from the year 2300.

Try drawing the same street using a higher camera. Just place the horizon line near the top of the frame. Use the same vanishing point and vertical start lines and start sketching.

TWO-POINT PERSPECTIVE INTERIORS

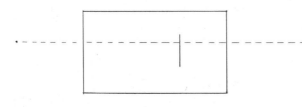

You will use this approach when you are setting up a shot that is looking into a corner of a room. It also is known as a 3/4 angle or raking shot.

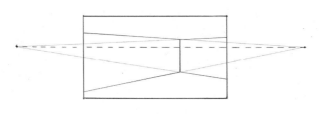

Start with a horizontal frame and visualize how far you are from the back wall or the corner of the space. As in the interior of the one-point perspective room, the back wall line needs to be drawn in before the horizon line is set. If you are looking deep into a large space, the line might cover only a fraction of the height of the frame. If you are in a smaller room, the line will be longer.

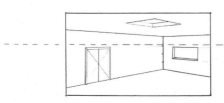

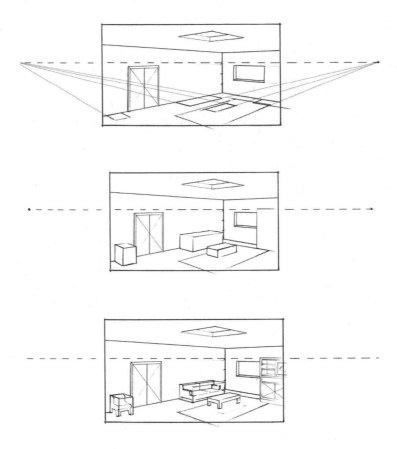

Place a vertical line in your frame and decide the height of the camera by drawing a horizon line through the frame. Place the two vanishing points on the horizon line, outside the frame itself. Now draw the lines that will describe the ceiling, floor, and walls. Use the vanishing points as pivots and draw *the left wall using the right vanishing point and the right wall using the left one*. This can be tricky to remember, but in two-point perspective you only use the right vanishing point to draw right-sided planes when you are drawing the outside of a box. When you are inside the box, you flip the orientation and use the opposite vanishing point.

This procedure may seem strange at first, but after drawing a few interiors, it will become second nature. Once the walls are drawn in, begin to furnish the room. Pop in a couple of windows, a door, and try a fireplace. Add a table, some chairs, and place a couple of standing figures in the scene. You can use the vanishing points to scale the figures in the space.

EXERCISE

Once you have gone through the preceding material, try to render this short shot list using the correct version of perspective and the appropriate horizon line. A student example is provided for reference.

I call this project the "Backwards Shot List," because you take a sequence that has already been shot and edited and create a shot list, working in the opposite of the normal progression.

1. Exterior day, Western town. High angle, frontal shot of a small 19th-century town. A wagon lies abandoned in the street.

2. Full shot of the saloon doors, a man waits to come through. Eye-level raking angle.

3. ECU of man's eyes, frontal.

4. Straight-on wide shot, eye-level of the front of saloon. Track left to follow man over to hotel.

STUDENT EXAMPLE

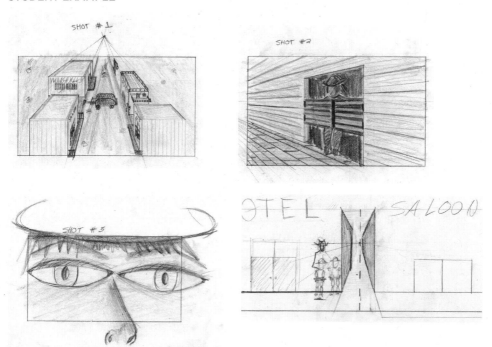

Drawings: Eric Thompson

BEYOND THE BOX

This chapter has offered some bare-bones techniques for adding space to your sketches. It is meant as a tool for those writers and directors who need a simple, visual language to communicate their shot ideas. For additional information on perspective, please refer to the excellent sources in the Bibliography (page 251) and consider taking a short class in linear perspective at your local community college or art academy.

Perspective sketch: Leo Kuter
Production designer: *Key Largo*, *Rio Bravo*

PORTFOLIO ON THE LOOSE

Two years after I arrived in Los Angeles, I had managed to put together enough work to fill a good-sized portfolio. This included storyboards, production sketches, and set photos from the films that I had decorated. I decided that it was time to introduce myself to a larger community of art directors and production designers. To this end, I invested in a beautiful leather-edged case with large plastic-covered pages inside. I made up captions, typed up a new resume and had large prints made of all my best set shots.

I called up the art directors I had already worked with and asked for the names of other art directors who might be looking to expand their crews. I set up seven or eight meetings over the course of two weeks and was set to begin the interview process when I decided to go downtown to show my new book to a friend. We were going to have dinner and since the portfolio was large and heavy and I was running late, I locked it in the trunk of my car. We finished about 9:30 and walked back to the lot. It was one of the outdoor lots common to downtown Los Angeles. The attendant had already gone home. We reached the car and I popped the lock. I will always remember the sight of that empty trunk. I had trouble breathing as I tried to take in what had happened. I even checked to see if I was dreaming. No such luck; the portfolio was gone. And this was not just my Los Angeles work, but photos of sets I had designed in New York, original set illustrations... everything.

Mildly stated, I was very upset. We began to comb the area looking in every dumpster for a three-block radius. I called the police and made a report, but they weren't helpful. I could only hope that whoever had the case would dump the contents and they would be recovered. But nothing ever turned up. And I had interviews with some of the top designers in town starting the next day and nothing to show.

When I returned home I began to comb through the "reject" pile for some photos and storyboards that I could cobble into a presentation format. I was desperate, just this side of defeated at the daunting task of redoing all my work, but between calls to coworkers for replacement photos and long hours at the drawing table, I managed to create a "portfolio version 2.0," which was in some ways better than its predecessor. Thereafter I vowed to never leave the portfolio in my car, never put original work in the book, and always have copies made of my drawings. I also realized that even when my most "valuable" professional possession was taken from me, I was able to go to my interviews and make a convincing presentation. They were hiring me, not my portfolio. In subsequent years I insisted, whenever possible, to meet with prospective employers personally, and not just leave a portfolio as some requested. Even if it was just to shake hands and say hello, there is power in connecting a person to the portfolio.

"On the first film I directed, I made drawings. I wanted to be very sure. I was uncertain of myself as far as the camera was concerned and I wanted to be sure not to fumble, not to get lost in the mechanical aspects of making a film. So I made drawings of every setup..."

—John Huston
Hollywood Voices
Director: *The Maltese Falcon*, T*he African Queen*

THE HUMAN FORM

This chapter will concentrate on the development of figure notation. The human figure is perhaps the most common element in film composition. Whether the shot is a close-up, a long shot, or a full-figure, chances are that there will be a human form somewhere inside the frame. Some of you will approach this challenge with little or no figure drawing experience. Others, myself included, come from a background in fine art and are accustomed to referring to live models as we draw. For those with limited or no drawing experience, this chapter will take you through some simple steps that will improve your ability to render natural-looking figures. For artists accustomed to using live models, the information will guide you toward simplifying your notion of the human body so that you can quickly render human forms using a simple internalized model instead of a complex live figure.

Our bodies are composed of over 200 bones and hundreds more muscles. Besides these basic biological traits, our forms carry marks of personality, gender, ethnicity, and individual history. That makes the human figure one of the most complex forms to render in a natural-looking manner.

> "For Duel the entire movie was storyboarded. I think that when you make an action film, especially a road picture, it's the best way to work, because it's very hard to pick up a script and sift through five hundred words of prose and then commit them to memory…. I felt that breaking the picture up and mapping it out would be easier for me."
>
> — Steven Spielberg
> Director: *Jaws, E.T., Schindler's List*

> "Don't try to do a complete drawing all at once. Spend all the time you can doodling with stick figures. They're the easiest way for you to get the action and position that you want for your characters."
>
> — Stan Lee
> *How to Draw Comics the Marvel Way*

That said, the director or writer who is using storyboards to help visualize his or her project needs to concentrate only on some of the fundamentals of the form.

MAIN ELEMENTS OF FIGURE COMMUNICATION:

> SCALE

> PROPORTION

> GESTURE

> THREE-DIMENSIONAL FORM (various approaches)

> SKELETAL FORM

> SIMPLE GEOMETRIC SHAPES

> STACKED ELLIPSES

The fine artist and illustrator have a different challenge. For them, the process involves simplifying a form they already understand in terms of its deep complexities. To accommodate the storyboard format, the network of interlaced shapes that make up the head, torso, and extremities of a human form will now need to be rendered on a relatively small scale, often no larger than 3" by 5". In addition, the presentation of light and shadow needs to be accomplished as quickly and accurately as possible.

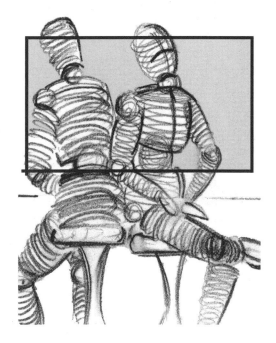

SIMPLIFIED FORMS

Sometimes a storyboard artist will get location or set model photos to use as reference, but most of the time you will find yourself working from overhead diagrams and shot descriptions. Many artists new to storyboarding find they have to develop a revised set of rendering skills that focus on mentally designing each shot before they begin to visualize it on paper.

When I came into the film industry, I had been working as a set designer for theater and as an artist who specialized in portraiture. When I began to work as a storyboard artist, it took me well over a year to internalize a generic human that I could call forth from my mind at will, having no external imagery for reference.

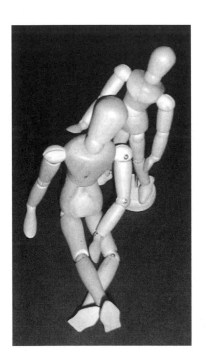

The first step for me was to acquire a 12"-high mannequin with moveable limbs. These can be found in most art and graphic supply stores. They usually are built with simple wooden shapes, an egg-like form for the head, a sphere for the neck pivot, a rounded trapezoid for the torso, and tapered cylinders for the arms and legs. There are no articulated fingers or facial features, just the basics.

The limbs, head, and torso are linked by a spring mechanism that allows you to pose the figure, and then lets the "body" maintain that shape after you release the limbs. By using an aspect ratio cutout, you can arrange the mannequin so that you can see the gesture of the figure in whichever scale you desire. You now have a visual reference from which to build your drawing.

This approach may sound time-consuming, but it's actually fun. There is a lovely element of play to this that will make the time pass quickly. Also, many people experience a higher level of achievement with a short amount of practice using this tool.

You cannot overestimate the importance of play in this process. Many of you stopped drawing, cut yourselves off from expressing the visual world, when your internal criticisms became too severe. Small children have a universal love of painting and drawing. It is inbred, just as the need to speak and to write comes with the desire to communicate about the world. Some of you will now be opening yourselves up to an ancient manner of expression. In the history of "scripting," the image predates the word.

In the preliminary storyboard image, remember:

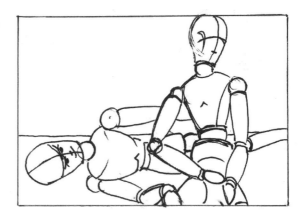

> Gesture Before Detail

> Three-Dimensional Figure in Space

> Simple Animation of Facial Expressions

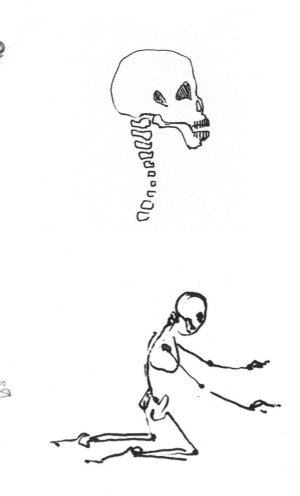

THE FIGURE

The focus here will be on three ways to quickly sketch the figure and communicate its gestures in space. Skeletons are the next step up from the beginner's stick-figure rendition of the human body. They can be created from some simple building blocks that are far easier to put together than a fully-clothed figure.

The next step up might be creating human forms from simple geometric shapes, such as cylinders and cubes. Stacked in proportion, this figure can be rotated and sketched more easily from memory than a true anatomical version.

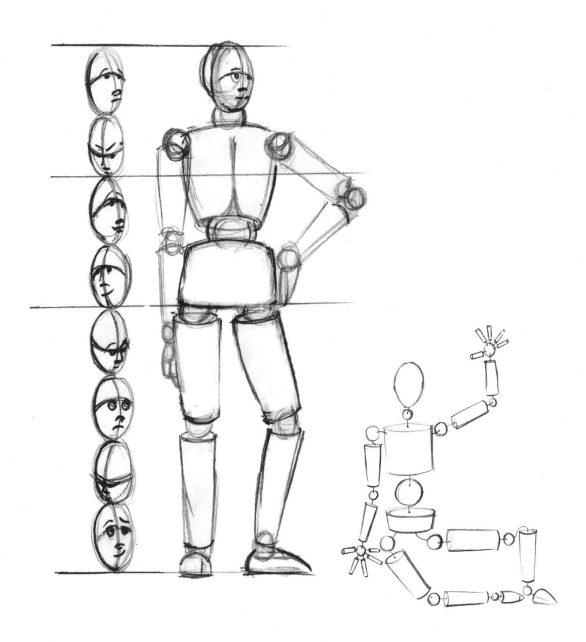

Stacked ellipses, which can be sketched as unbroken spirals, can also be helpful in getting the figure into three dimensions. Remember, you are attempting to *refer* to human movement and positioning, not faithfully *reproduce* it.

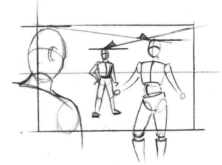

USE VANISHING POINTS TO LINE UP THE TOPS OF HEADS.

TRY SKETCHING MANNEQUINS IN VARIOUS POSITIONS.

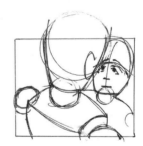

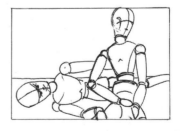

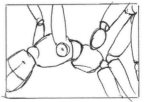

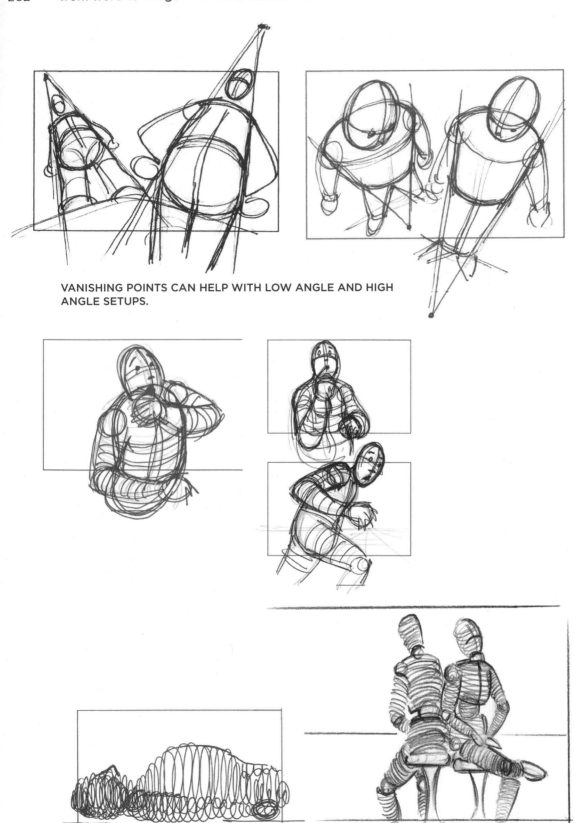

VANISHING POINTS CAN HELP WITH LOW ANGLE AND HIGH
ANGLE SETUPS.

THE HEAD

It's said that as we age, our face shows the life we have lived. Of all the parts that make up our bodies, the head has attracted the most attention. It is the site of the "windows to our souls," the plane on which our expressions reflect our emotional lives. It can communicate our feelings, which are at times a counterpoint to our words.

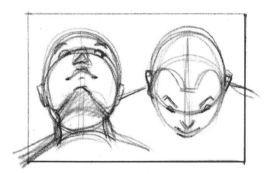 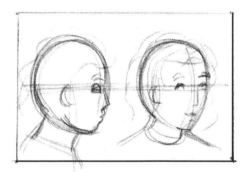

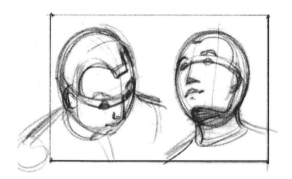 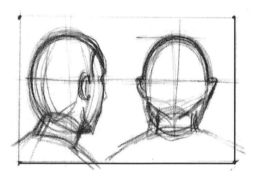

Let's start with the egg. An egg on end, with the thicker end toward the sky, is a good place to start in the rendering of a head.

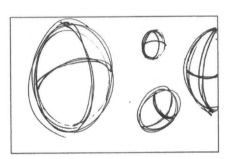

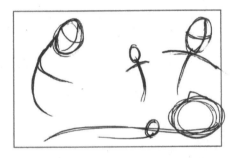

A SIMPLE "EGG" HEAD AND A SPINE-LINE CAN GIVE GESTURE TO A BASIC FIGURE.

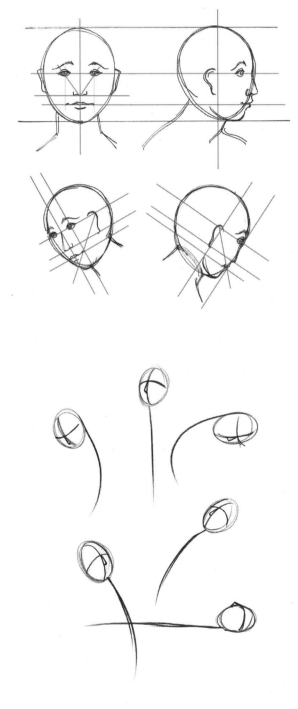

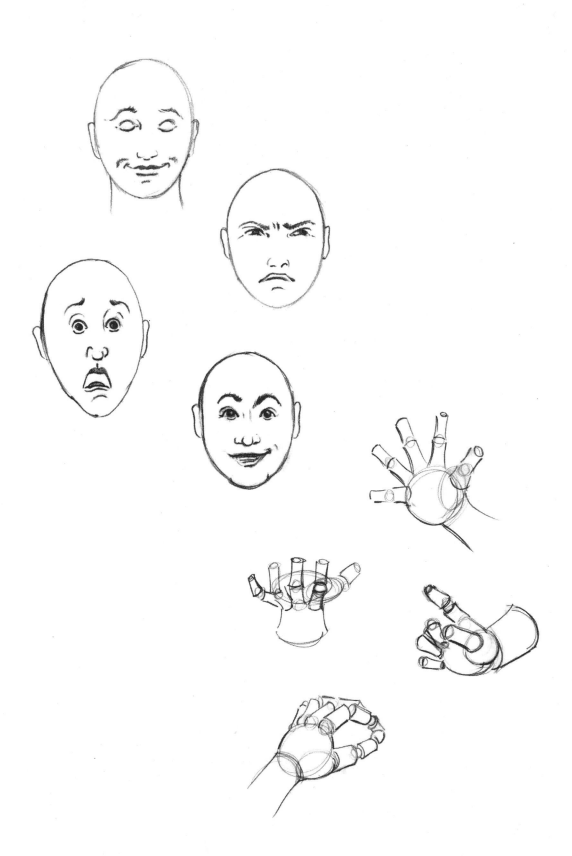

SUMMARY

The important thing to remember is that **this process needs to focus on experimentation, not "success" and "failure"** as viewed through the comparison of your drawings to the art of professional illustrators. As directors and writers you are looking for a shorthand style to effectively communicate your ideas on blocking and composition. It's not that you "can't draw" or that you are missing some "talent" that other people seem to be born with. It's just that you need to sharpen a skill that has been long dormant.

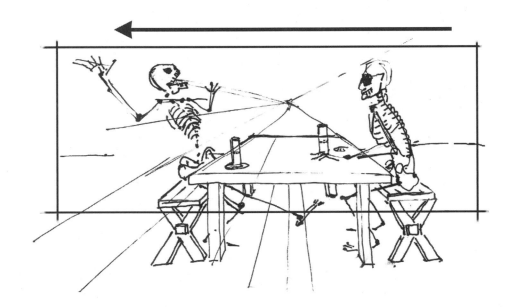

SEE WHAT YOU CAN COME UP WITH

I was hired to storyboard a feature for a first-time director. He had worked in music videos and commercials and had a great visual flair. I arrived for our first meeting and was asked to wait outside his office, because he was busy interviewing designers. I read the newspapers. I went for coffee. His assistant apologized, and I went to lunch. That afternoon he was busy with casting. Finally he had a break in his schedule, and I was offered a seat across from his desk. He handed me a script and asked me to look at couple of scenes and get back to him when I had something for him to look at. No conversation, no advice guidance of any kind. We worked together in this way for a few weeks. I would stop by to drop off drawings and get a new assignment. He would glance at the work and run off for another casting session. I had a good time drawing up the boards, but never made much of a connection with the director or figured out how he was planning to use the information. When I saw the completed film, it was clear that he didn't use the boards at all.

People use the boards in many ways. Sometimes they are a way to involve another sensibility into the visual mix. Sometimes they are created just to satisfy the demands of an off-site producing organization. It's a good idea to determine where the boards are heading and what purpose they will be put to before you start the process.

Drawing: Anton Grot
Production designer: *Little
Caesar, Gold Diggers of 1933,
Mildred Pierce*

"Artists need a full, convertible
portfolio. Producers and directors
can have tunnel vision when it
comes to visualizing their project.
Artists can be typecast just like
actors and you need examples
from all genres to show to prospective employers."

—Phillip Mittel
Motion Artists Agency

GETTING A GIG

When I first arrived in Los Angeles, I knew a total of three people who worked in the industry. I called each one of them and reminded them that they were, in part, responsible for my making the move. I was fortunate. Work came only two days later, constructing props and painting sets for a special effects company. I had made it clear that I was willing to do *anything*.

For the next two years I took everything that came my way in terms of work. I scattered beef brains at 3 a.m. on a butcher's set floor. Shoveled cow poop in a pasture to clear a picnic set. Drove 80 mph in a rainstorm to replace a neon fixture in a bar location. I worked on films with scripts that included scenes I would never want to see in the theater. It was all bankable experience. I said yes to everything and learned skills on the fly. Whenever I was asked if I could do something that I didn't really know how to do, I tried to flash a confident smile and then went about learning how to do it, if not brilliantly, at least competently.

Most of my work came through word of mouth. If a gig went well, I tried to stay in touch with my coworkers and made sure they knew how to reach me if and when another project came along. In addition, I expanded my storyboard portfolio by working with young directors just finishing school or breaking into the business. This means that I found myself on very low-budget and even no-budget projects, but I was able to forge new relationships and create boards that were based on real-world experiences rather than theoretic exercises.

In Los Angeles there are numerous film schools and university departments that are constantly churning out graduates in directing and cinematography. These filmmakers often need assistance in visualizing their projects. There are fewer storyboard artists than directing novices. I printed up a flyer with examples of my work and a contact number and posted them at the American Film Institute and UCLA. Within a few weeks I had formed relationships with two directors and was storyboarding their films. With that expanded portfolio, I then went around introducing myself to a series of production houses.

STRATEGY

First you need to identify those businesses in your area that might have a need for storyboards or other types of previsualization documents. Make a list of:

> Film schools

> Universities that have departments of film, communication, or drama

> Video production houses — especially those that produce music videos

> Advertising agencies

> CD-ROM and DVD development companies

> Website designers who use motion graphics

INTERNSHIPS

The above list can all be excellent places to start introducing yourself. If you can afford to work as an intern for a short while, then draft a proposal that will show best what you have to offer. Often these internships turn into paid work if you can demonstrate to the company that you can meet deadlines and improve their work environment. One word of warning, though: If you accept an internship position, be very clear as to the parameters of what you are willing to offer in terms of time. Two months is reasonable, two years is not. Make this clear up front so there will be no misunderstanding when you are ready to move on (or up).

PORTFOLIOS

Because of the ease of website development, consider creating an online portfolio of your work and biographical credits. Purchase a domain name with your business name or given name as the primary url and develop a digital portfolio that can be accessed by anyone anywhere. (Check out the great examples of artist sites in Appendix III, Websites with Visualization Content, page 237.) If this outlay is beyond your means at this time, then consider creating a Flickr account or a blog that will feature your work. Spend some time tweaking your images in Photoshop so they read well in a digital format. I would caution against listing your fees online — leaving this topic open will give yourself some "wiggle room" in negotiations.

Also, when selecting images for your site, you can show a variety of work, from loose pencil sketches to highly developed production illustrations. Let a prospective client see your flexibility and a body of work that is reflective of the entire spectrum of your abilities. Remember, some directors are looking for quick sketches and others for polished illustrations.

FLAT-FEE ARRANGEMENT

Another situation that you may be offered early in your career is the flat-fee arrangement. In this setup you will be paid a fixed amount to do the job (e.g., a 20-minute dramatic script being produced for the film festival circuit). This can often be a great way to meet people with more experience and good connections to future work. However, the flip side is that you are trading your work on a script for a set, usually limited, amount of money. If there are extensive changes to the script or other revisions, you may find yourself working ad infinitum on what you thought was going to be a 10-day gig.

That was my position on my first paid job. For room, board, and a small flat fee, I agreed to storyboard an entire feature. I later calculated that I had been paid less than the rental on one of the klieg lights. I do not regret a moment. It was trial by fire (or ice, in that chilly Cape Cod autumn), and I happily showed up on the set each day to draw, move furniture, or do whatever else that might cross the production designer's mind that day. When I signed my contract, though, I somehow had enough sense to have a clause that included an ending date. In other words, I said yes to the flat fee, but only until the tenth of December, which was the estimated last day of shooting. And, as often happens, shooting went over the expected finish day. From that day on, if they wanted a storyboard artist on the set, they needed to pay an additional fee. Was it much money? Of course not. Did it keep the relationship clean between the producers and me? Absolutely, because no one needed to ask a favor.

SLIDING SCALE

Once I reached a state in my working life where I felt I could pick and choose a bit, I realized that there was an inverse relationship between content and money. In other words, for a commercial that had basically no content aside from the product it was seeking to advertise, I was offered a high fee. On the other hand, the small, independent features that I yearned to be involved with often didn't have very much money for preproduction expenses. My solution was to institute a sliding scale for my services that ensured the ad agencies and TV studios paid top prices while independent films and small music videos were charged a reduced rate.

This approach is not for everyone, and if you are working through an agent, he or she may not like this arrangement at all. But for me it was a solution to my own desire to stay available for small, edgy projects that couldn't necessarily afford my going fees.

AGENCIES

Once your career is underway and you have a solid portfolio of work to present, you might want to consider finding an agent. There are a number of issues involved with this type of representation.

Do you want to be on call every day, all day? Many agents require that you carry a beeper and be available at a call's notice. If you are a fast-track person, this will suit your pace; but if you want to carve out a part-time niche for yourself, it may not be a good fit.

There are many reasons to have an agent. Your agent can act as a go-between in your contract negotiations. This can often lead to higher day rates and better fringe benefits, such as the use of a car on location or overtime pay. They will be responsible for paying you rather than the production house or ad agency. This can alleviate the headache of tardy payments for work done months before.

Another reason to use an agent is for their depth of connections within the industry. It's their job to have information regarding all the current and future productions in your area.

While you are busy working on a show, they will be looking out for your next gig. Some agents will even work as career managers, counseling you on which productions will add the most interest to your portfolio or setting up meetings with hot new directors who may be getting their first features in the coming months.

"What I look for in a portfolio is diversity. If you only want to do film, then the supply and demand will make it more difficult to work all the time. I need to see how tight an artist can work. I get calls for loose drawings from some production houses, but in order to send an artist every day, I need him to be able to work on many levels of polish. You need to look at the best artists out there and try to come up to their standards. We have lots of artists that come from a background in comic book art as well as classically trained illustrators. We also look for a solid understanding of film language."

—Mark Miller
   Founder of Famous
   Frames, an agency that
   handles storyboard
   artists and illustrators

An agency will typically take a 25% cut out of the artist's fee, although that can be reduced over time if the artist stays with the agency and works regularly. Even with this cut, agencies can often negotiate higher fees, so the artist can find more in his or her pocket in the end. Some agencies ask for an exclusive contract, while others will allow outside work. These points are usually decided on a case-by-case basis. If you have many good contacts within your industry, an agent may not be able to offer you enough to make the relationship worthwhile. But if you are an artist who would rather not spend time with the details of business, then an agent may be the way to go.

"If you have a portfolio of Westerns, they probably won't hire you for a sci-fi film. Also, it helps to have work using a variety of media such as pencil, marker, and computer. I look for great skills in drawing as well as a sharp sense of designing the frame. Many of our artists trained as transportation designers before transferring into entertainment design. Now they do it all: theme parks, creatures, and special effects as well as traditional film."

— Phillip Mittel
    Founder of Motion
    Artists, an agency
    that places artists,
    production designers,
    concept artists, and
    digital designers

If you're not sure whether going through an agency is right for you, ask yourself a few questions:

Does the agency require that all the work you book be funneled through them and that they get a piece of it, even if the job came through your own connections?

How quickly will they pay you for your work? Some agencies work on a 30-day net, some take even longer to get you your wages. On the other hand, if you are hired directly by a production company, the checks are usually cut on a weekly or bi-weekly schedule.

Do you want the security of the agency dealing directly with the production company? You are then saved from having to make your own contracts and the worry of — if the company is unknown to you — whether it will honor its commitments.

Do you like being part of a team and having someone else closely involved with the path of your career? If so, then an agent might fit well into your plan. If you are by nature a loner and value autonomy, then you might want to stay independent and make your own connections.

UNIONS

The union for illustrators and matte artists is IATSE (International Alliance of Theater and Employees) Local 800 (formerly #790). The original guild was founded in 1945, at the end of the war, when many returning servicemen were looking for employment in the booming film industry. As of publication, the illustrators have been folded into local 800, with the art directors and other artists. As stated on their website (www.artdirectors.org), "Local 800 is an international union, which exclusively represents employees in the entertainment industry, spanning the United States and Canada with more than 104,000 members. Local 800 is comprised of Art Directors, Graphic Artists, Illustrators, Matte Artists, Model Makers, Scenic Artists, Set Designers and Title Artists."

If you are working under a union contract, you are assured of receiving health insurance, pension, and other benefits rarely offered to freelancers or artists working as independent contractors. Because most storyboard work these days is available on a freelance basis (as of the end of the studio era), many artists want to work as a part of a group that sets wage minimums, working conditions, and offers some of the options, like health coverage, that freelance workers often lack.

THE CATCH (22, that is...)

In order to join the union, you need to have worked 30 days on a union production. In order to work on a union production, you usually need to be in the union. Aye, there's the rub. This strange set of circumstances can be overcome in a few different ways. First, once all the members on the union roster are working, a production may hire anyone they wish to fill the position of illustrator or storyboard artist. This situation is rare, but occasionally the roster has 100% employment of eligible artists, and non-union workers may be hired onto a union signatory production.

You can also gain entrance by working a non-union film that becomes union. All your hours, even those worked before the union contract, become union hours, and if you've got thirty days at the end of production, you will be "grandfathered" onto the roster.

There is a new way to become a member, which is to work 30 days on a signatory of AICP, the Alliance of Commercial Producers. Once you have those days, you can register with an organization called Contract Services, which keeps records of your days worked, and after another 90 days on a signatory production you will be admitted to the union.

Local 800 of IATSE is a useful resource for artists who live and work in areas where IATSE is active. Aside from the media centers of Los Angeles and New York, it will probably not be necessary to join in order to obtain a position on a crew.

FREELANCE OR TEAM PLAYER?

From the time I graduated college until I took my first position as a teacher, I worked as a freelance designer and illustrator for 14 years. Every few months I changed jobs, met new coworkers, and explored challenges of designing for theater and film that I could not have imagined before I was faced with solving them. Under these conditions I thrived. It's not for everyone. Here's a quick checklist:

Roller coasters	Row boats
Hotel rooms	Home-cooked meals
Surprise parties	Casual Fridays
Spontaneity	Long-range planning
Shifting deadlines	Staying on schedule

If the items on the left annoy or frustrate you, consider looking for in-house employment. If you can't get enough of those loop-de-loops and can laugh at the shifting sands, then you might have a freelance temperament.

SUMMARY

In the end, how you structure your entry into the art and business of preproduction visualization should be based on individual needs. Is there a medium that you are attracted to more than the rest? How much do you want to work, and do you want to travel for extended periods of time? Do you have an independent character or do you like being one of an ongoing team? All these issues can inform the path you take once your career is underway. Until then, take what comes and keep your eyes open for any opportunity that might cross your path.

SIGNING OFF...

This journey has taken us through the world of representation and abstraction, imagery and the written word in an effort to guide and assist you in communicating your inner vision. Whether you keep your pre-viz documents to yourself or publish them for all the world to see, I hope that the ideas and the tools in these chapters will aid you in your creative process. The making of a film, video, or CD-ROM can be an expansive challenge. Let yourself play with new ways of seeing and your stories will take on new forms of expression.

Thanks for your time and attention.

iMindMap
www.tonybuzan.com

This non-linear brainstorming program is a great tool not only for getting storyboard ideas flowing but also for capturing notions about any multi-dimensional project. Used for trip planning, book outlines, history homework, and many other tasks, this package has endless uses. An intuitive interface and a supportive website allow beginning users to create intricate Mind-Maps after negotiating an easy-to master learning curve.

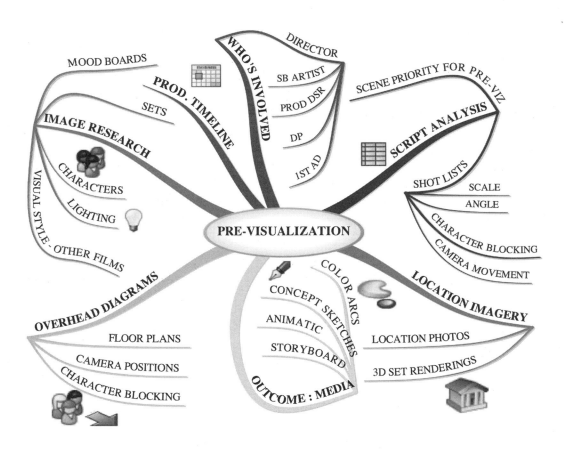

Frame Forge 3D
www.frameforge3d.com

This entry into the digital storyboard market takes computer-aided pre-viz into a world of three dimensions. Sets can be quickly blocked out in the easy-to-use 3D engine, props and figures added and cameras placed to capture the exact angle and framing of your choice. You can then save frames and arrange them in sequence, create an animatic and even have the software create "tween" shots so you can see how your camera moves will appear. This package is a lot of fun to work with — very intuitive and you get usable frames with relatively little investment of time. Although you do not have intricate texturing and lighting options of full 3D programs like Maya, there is enough variety in the pre-loaded set and character pieces to satisfy many production needs. Once you have created an environment and set the figures (you can change expression and gesture), manipulating the camera and snapping off shots is a speedy process.

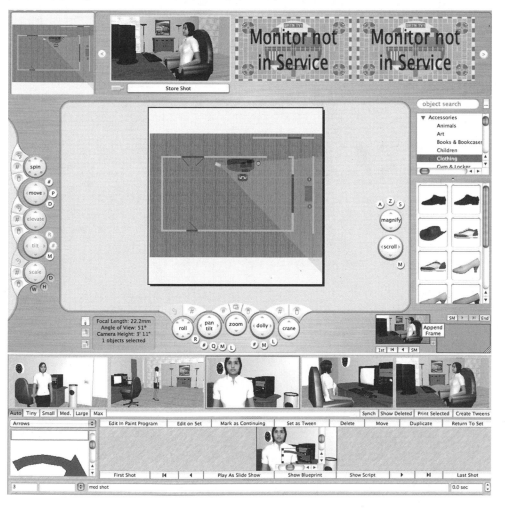

Toon Boom Storyboard and Storyboard Pro
www.toonboom.com

With extended animatic capabilities and simple drawing functions, this package is geared toward beginning as well as more advanced animators. That doesn't mean that live action directors, DPs, and conceptual artists won't find it useful as well. The aspect ratio is variable and the vector-based drawing tools make this a good presentation tool for planning motion graphic projects. You can import scripts to select and drag caption text into preformatted text boxes that can be viewed in a timeline along with storyboard frames. You can also import sound files and mix them with pictures as you work on timing your presentation.

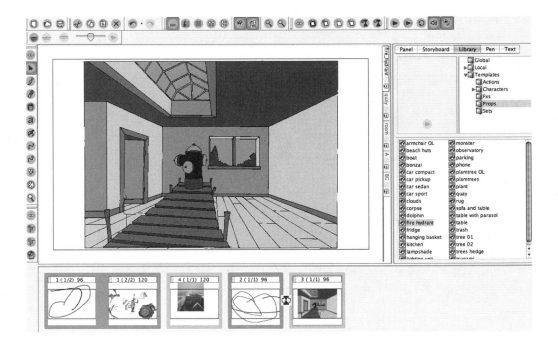

The package includes a modest library of diagrams, sets, and characters to enhance frame design and get you started. I found the easy-to-use interface allowed for quick short animations and camera movement. This is a good choice for those who already have boards drawn out and want to add some additional layers and movement to their presentations.

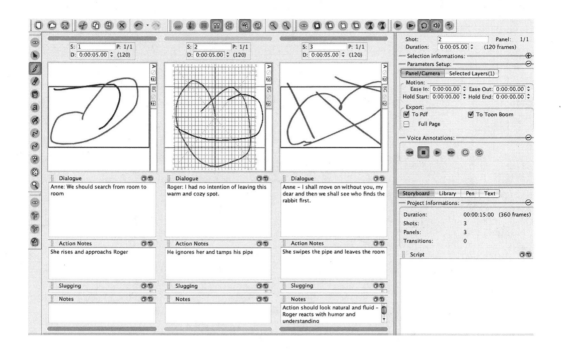

StoryBoard Quick 6
www.PowerProductions.com

This software package has a simple interface and a library of simple backgrounds, props, and figures that allows rapid development of basic boards. The current version which was released in 2009 has much improved image quality from its predecessor, but the set that is included in the basic package is somewhat limited (e.g., desk, yes; trash can, no). When you open a new project you are given a choice of aspect ratios, and once you have created frames, you can edit them in a useful overview window. The figure rotation button is a useful tool that allows you to chose an alternate perspective of a figure you have already placed in the frame without going back to the character menu.

Once you have selected a background, props, and characters for a frame, you have limited options regarding manipulation. You can scale them, move the layers back and forward, and change a character's clothing, skin and hair color. But you cannot erase a piece of a layer, say, if you want a character to seem as if they are entering from a door in the background. To achieve this you must import your own images that have been created with an alpha layer, which will preserve transparent areas.

Storyboard Artist

This package, also from PowerProductions, adds professional touches along with its heftier price tag. With a deeper image library (including facial expressions), additional drawing tools, more intricate camera movements and more access to manipulate the timeframe tool, this program is useful for commercial houses that want to develop presentation animations, production studios, and more advanced film students.

1. ***20000 Leagues Under the Sea*** (1954)
   (Special Edition)
   Director: Richard Fleischer
   Label: Walt Disney Home Video
   Release Date: 2003-05-20
   Supplements: Storyboard-to-scene comparison.

2. ***39 Steps, The*** (1935)
   Director: Alfred Hitchcock
   Label: Criterion Collection
   Release Date: 1999-11-02
   Supplements: Original production design drawings.

3. ***Abyss, The*** (1989)
   (Special Edition)
   Director: James Cameron
   Label: 20th Century Fox
   Release Date: 2003-02-11
   Supplements: DVD-ROM script and storyboard-to-screen comparison.

4. ***Alexander Nevsky*** (1938); ***Ivan the Terrible, Parts 1 & 2*** (1944)
   Eisenstein – The Sound Years (1947)
   Director: Sergei M. Eisenstein
   Label: Criterion Collection
   Release Date: 2001-04-24
   Supplements: *Alexander Nevsky* sketches and storyboards; *Ivan The Terrible*, *Parts 1 and 2*, sketches and storyboards.

5. ***Alice in Wonderland*** (1951)
   Directors: Clyde Geronimi; Wilfred Jackson; Hamilton Luske
   Label: Walt Disney Home Video
   Release Date: 2004-01-27
   Supplements: Deleted storyboard concept: "Alice Daydreams in the Park."

6. ***Alien*** (1979)
   (The Director's Cut)
   Director: Ridley Scott
   Label: 20th Century Fox
   Release Date: 2004-01-06
   Supplements: "Ridleygrams" (original thumbnails and notes), storyboard archive, "Art of *Alien*" (Cobb, Foss, Giger, Moebius).

7. ***Alien³*** (1992)
    (Two-Disc Collector's Edition)
    Director: David Fincher
    Label: 20th Century Fox
    Release Date: 2004-01-06
    Supplements: Preproduction: "The Art of Aceron" (conceptual art portfolio), preproduction part III featurette, storyboards, "Art of Fiorina," "Xeno-Erotic" (H.R. Giger's redesign featurette).

8. ***Amélie*** (2001) (***Le Fabuleux destin d'Amélie Poulain***)
    Director: Jean-Pierre Jeunet
    Label: Miramax Home Entertainment
    Release Date: 2002-07-16
    Supplements: Storyboard comparison.

9. ***American Beauty*** (1999)
    (Widescreen Edition)
    Director: Sam Mendes
    Label: DreamWorks
    Release Date: 2000-10-24
    Supplements: Storyboard presentation with Sam Mendes and Director of Photography Conrad L. Hall.

10. ***Artificial Intelligence: AI*** (2001)
    (Widescreen Two-Disc Special Edition)
    Director: Steven Spielberg
    Label: Universal Studios
    Release Date: 2002-03-05
    Supplements: Storyboard sequences.

11. ***Bad Boys II*** (2003)
    Director: Michael Bay
    Label: Columbia
    Release Date: 2003-12-09
    Supplements: Six sequence breakdowns, including on-the-set footage, storyboards, and scripts.

12. ***Basic Instinct*** (1992)
    (Director's Cut – Ultimate Edition)
    Director: Paul Verhoeven
    Label: Lionsgate
    Release Date: 2006-03-14
    Supplements: Storyboard comparisons.

13. *Beautiful Mind, A* (2001)
    (Widescreen Awards Edition)
    Director: Ron Howard
    Label: Universal Studios
    Release Date: 2004-06-01
    Supplements: Storyboards to final feature comparison.

14. *Ben-Hur* (1959)
    (Four-Disc Collector's Edition)
    Director: William Wyler
    Label: Warner Home Video
    Release Date: 2005-09-13
    Supplements: "Ben-Hur: A Journey Through Pictures," new audiovisual
    recreation of the film via stills, storyboards, sketches, music and dialogue.

15. *Birds, The* (1963)
    (Collector's Edition)
    Director: Alfred Hitchcock
    Label: Universal
    Release Date: 2000-03-28
    Supplements: Storyboard sequence and newsreel.

16. *Brazil* (1985)
    (The Criterion Collection)
    Director: Terry Gilliam
    Label: Criterion Collection
    Release Date: 1999-07-13
    Supplements: Terry Gilliam's original dream sequences, in storyboards,
    include hundreds of shots that never made it to the screen.

17. *Bug's Life, A* (1998)
    (Two-Disc Collector's Edition)
    Directors: John Lasseter; Andrew Stanton
    Label: Buena Vista Home Entertainment
    Release Date: 2003-05-27
    Supplements: Storyboard-to-final film split-screen comparison.

18. *Cinderella* (1950)
    (Two-Disc Special Edition)
    Directors: Clyde Geronimi; Wilfred Jackson; Hamilton Luske
    Studio: Walt Disney Home Entertainment
    Release Date: 2005-10-04
    Supplements: Storyboard to film comparison: the opening sequence.

19. ***Citizen Kane*** (1941)
    (Two-Disc Special Edition)
    Director: Orson Welles
    Label: Warner Home Video
    Release Date: 2001-09-25
    Supplements: Gallery of storyboards, rare photos, alternate ad campaign, studio and personal correspondence, call sheets, and other memorabilia.

20. ***City of Lost Children, The*** (1995) (La Cité des enfants perdus)
    (Special Edition)
    Directors: Marc Caro, Jean-Pierre Jeunet
    Label: Columbia Tristar Home Video
    Release Date: 1999-10-19
    Supplements: Production sketch gallery.

21. ***Cliffhanger*** (1993)
    (Collector's Edition)
    Director: Renny Harlin
    Label: Columbia Tristar
    Release Date: 2000-06-13
    Supplements: Three storyboard comparisons.

22. ***Cold Mountain*** (2003)
    (Two-Disc Collector's Edition)
    Director: Anthony Minghella
    Label: Miramax Films
    Release Date: 2004-06-29
    Supplements: Storyboard comparisons of three scenes.

23. ***Dark Crystal, The*** (1982)
    (Collector's Edition Boxed Set)
    Directors: Jim Henson; Frank Oz; Gary Kurtz
    Label: Columbia
    Release Date: 2003-11-25
    Supplements: Henson storyboards and character drawings.

24. ***Dead Ringers*** (1988)
    Director: David Cronenberg
    Label: Criterion Collection
    Release Date: 1998-10-14
    Supplements: The original designs for the opening credit sequence, drawings and photographs of the medical instruments, and sculptures designed for the movie.

25. **Die Another Day** (2002)
    (Widescreen Special Edition)
    Director: Lee Tamahori
    Label: MGM
    Release Date: 2003-06-03
    Supplements: Storyboard-to-final-shot comparisons for key scenes.

26. **Die Hard 2: Die Harder** (1990)
    (Special Edition)
    Director: Renny Harlin
    Label: 20th Century Fox
    Release Date: 2001-07-10
    Supplements: Behind-the-scenes and storyboards.

27. **Die Hard: With a Vengeance** (1995)
    (Special Edition)
    Director: John McTiernan
    Label: 20th Century Fox
    Release Date: 2001-07-10
    Supplements: Storyboards.

28. **Do The Right Thing** (1989)
    Label: Criterion Collection
    Director: Spike Lee
    Release Date: 2001-02-20
    Supplements: Original storyboards for the riot sequence, plus a film-to-storyboard comparison.

29. **Dogma** (1999)
    (Special Edition)
    Director: Kevin Smith
    Label: Columbia Tristar
    Release Date: 2001-06-26
    Supplements: Complete set of storyboards from three major scenes.

30. **Donnie Darko** (2001)
    (The Director's Cut: Two-Disc Special Edition)
    Director: Richard Kelly
    Label: 20th Century Fox
    Release Date: 2005-02-15
    Supplements: Storyboard-to-screen featurette.

31. *Duellists, The* (1977)
    Director: Ridley Scott
    Label: Paramount
    Release Date: 2002-12-03
    Supplements: Storyboards.

32. *Eragon* (2006)
    (Two-Disc Special Edition)
    Director: Stefen Fangmeier
    Label: 20th Century Fox
    Release Date: 2007-03-20
    Supplements: Original storyboards; "Chapter One: Realizing Alagaesia"
    (focusing on storyboards, location scouting, and character design);
    "Vision of Eragon: Conceptual Art Gallery."

33. *Exorcist, The* (1973)
    (25th Anniversary Special Edition)
    Director: William Friedkin
    Label: Warner Home Video
    Release Date: 1998-12-01
    Supplements: DVD-exclusive documentary featurette of the movie's
    storyboards and production.

34. *Family Plot* (1976)
    Director: Alfred Hitchcock
    Label: Universal Studios
    Release Date: 2001-03-06
    Supplements: Storyboards: the chase scene.

35. *Fantasia* (1940)
    (Special 60th Anniversary Edition)
    Directors: James Algar; Samuel Armstrong; Ford Beebe; Norman
    Ferguson; Jim Handley; T. Hee; Wilfred Jackson; Hamilton Luske; Bill
    Roberts; Paul Satterfield.
    Label: Walt Disney
    Release Date: 2000-11-14
    Supplements: In-depth exploration of segments, Including story-
    boards, concept art, and character designs.

36. *Fantastic Voyage* (1966)
(Special Edition)
Director: Richard Fleischer
Label: 20th Century Fox
Release Date: 2007-06-05
Supplements: Whirlpool Scene: storyboard-to-scene comparison; deleted scene: script-to-storyboard; storyboards: pre-miniaturization sequence.

37. *Fight Club* (1999)
(Two-Disc Collector's Edition)
Director: David Fincher
Label: 20th Century Fox
Release Date: 2000-06-06
Supplements: Still galleries: set design stills, costume stills, original sketches, oil paintings, storyboards, publicity stills, lobby cards and production stills.

38. *Final Fantasy: The Spirits Within* (2001)
(Special Edition)
Directors: Hironobu Sakaguchi; Moto Sakakibara
Label: Columbia Tri-Star
Release Date: 2001-10-23
Supplements: Storyboard/playblast selects of the film with optional filmmaker commentary or subtitled factoids

39. *Fog, The* (1980)
Director: John Carpenter
Label: MGM
Release Date: 2002-08-27
Supplements: Storyboard to film comparison.

40. *French Connection, The* (1971)
(Collection Box Set: 1 & 2)
Director: William Friedkin
Label: 20th Century Fox
Release Date: 2001-09-25
Supplements: Storyboard gallery.

41. *From Russia with Love* (1963)
(Special Edition)
Director: Terence Young
Label: MGM
Release Date: 2000-10-17
Supplements: Animated storyboard sequence.

42. *Ghost Busters* (1984)
     Director: Ivan Reitman
     Label: Columbia/Tristar
     Release Date: 2002-02-05
     Supplements: Storyboards with split-screen comparison.

43. *Gladiator* (2000)
     (Three-Disc Extended Edition)
     Director: Ridley Scott
     Studio: DreamWorks Video
     Release Date: 2005-08-23
     Supplements: Disc Three: behind the scenes production design fea-
     turette and gallery; storyboard demonstrations, comparisons and gal-
     lery; "Ridleygrams": Ridley Scott's own sketches of "Maximus' Journey";
     costume design gallery.

44. *Godfather, The* (1972); *The Godfather: Part II* (1974); *The Godfather:
     Part III* (1990)
     (*The Godfather* DVD Collection)
     Director: Francis Ford Coppola
     Label: Paramount
     Release Date: 2001-10-09
     Supplements: Production stills and storyboards.

45. *Gremlins* (1984)
     (Special Edition)
     Director: Joe Dante
     Label: Warner Home Video
     Release Date: 2002-08-20
     Supplements: Photo/storyboard gallery.

46. *Grudge, The* (2004)
     (Unrated Director's Cut)
     Director: Takashi Shimizu
     Studio: Sony Pictures
     Release Date: 2005-05-17
     Supplements: "Sights and Sounds: The Storyboard Art of Takashi Shimizu."

47. *Hills Have Eyes, The* (1977)
     (Two-Disc Edition)
     Director: Wes Craven
     Studio: Vanguard
     Release Date: 2003-09-23
     Supplements: Original storyboard art.

48. *Independence Day* (1996)
    (Two-Disc Collector's Edition)
    Director: Roland Emmerich
    Label: 20th Century Fox
    Release Date: 2003-09-23
    Supplements: Production stills gallery, storyboards gallery, and concept art gallery.

49. *Ivan the Terrible*, *Parts 1 & 2* (1944); *Alexander Nevsky* (1938)
    Eisenstein – The Sound Years (1947)
    Director: Sergei M. Eisenstein
    Label: Criterion Collection
    Release Date: 2001-04-24
    Supplements: *Alexander Nevsky* sketches and storyboards; *Ivan The Terrible, Parts 1 and 2*, sketches and storyboards.

50. *Jaws* (1975)
    (30th Anniversary Edition)
    Director: Steven Spielberg
    Label: Universal Studios
    Release Date: 2005-06-14
    Supplements: *Jaws* archives: storyboards, production photos, and marketing materials.

51. *Jumanji* (1995)
    (Collector's Series)
    Director: Joe Johnston
    Label: Columbia Tristar Home Video
    Release Date: 2000-01-25
    Supplements: Storyboards; production design documentary.

52. *Jurassic Park* (1993)
    (Widescreen Collector's Edition)
    Director: Steven Spielberg
    Label: Universal
    Release Date: 2000-10-10
    Supplements: Storyboards.

53. *Jurassic Park III* (2001)
    (Widescreen Collector's Edition)
    Director: Joe Johnston
    Label: Universal
    Release Date: 2001-12-11
    Supplements: Storyboard sequences.

54. ***Land of the Dead*** (2005)
    (Unrated Edition)
    Director: George A. Romero
    Label: Universal
    Release Date: 2005-10-18
    Supplements: "Bringing the Storyboards to Life."

55. ***Lord of the Rings: The Fellowship of the Ring, The*** (2001)
    (Platinum Series Special Extended Edition)
    Director: Peter Jackson
    Label: New Line
    Release Date: 2002-11-12
    Supplements: Storyboards to previsualization; footage from early
    meetings, moving storyboards, and previsualization reels.

56. ***Lord of the Rings: The Two Towers, The*** (2002)
    (Platinum Series Special Extended Edition)
    Director: Peter Jackson
    Label: New Line Home Video
    Release Date: 2003-11-18
    Supplements: Storyboards to previsualization.

57. ***Lost in La Mancha*** (2002)
    Directors: Keith Fulton; Louis Pepe
    Label: A&E Home Video
    Release Date: 2003-06-24
    Supplements: Storyboards, production stills, and costume designs
    from "The Man Who Killed Don Quixote."

58. ***Lost World: Jurassic Park, The*** (1997)
    (Widescreen Collector's Edition)
    Director: Steven Spielberg
    Label: Universal
    Release Date: 2000-10-10
    Supplements: Illustrations and conceptual drawings; storyboards and
    models.

59. ***Monsters, Inc.*** (2001)
    (Two-Disc Collector's Edition)
    Directors: Pete Docter; David Silverman; Lee Unkrich
    Label: Walt Disney Home Video
    Release Date: 2002-09-17
    Supplements: Film to storyboard comparisons.

60. *Nausicaä of the Valley of the Wind* (1984) (*Kaze no tani no Naushika*)
     Director: Hayao Miyazaki
     Label: Buena Vista Home Entertainment
     Release Date: 2005-02-22
     Supplements: Complete storyboards.

61. *Nightmare Before Christmas, The* (1993)
     (Special Edition)
     Director: Henry Selick
     Label: Buena Vista
     Release Date: 2000-10-03
     Supplements: Deleted footage: animated sequences and storyboards
     not used in the final film.

62. *Rififi* (1955) (*Du rififi chez les hommes*)
     (Criterion Collection)
     Director: Jules Dassin
     Label: HOME VISION
     Release Date: 2001-04-24
     Supplements: Production design drawings and stills.

63. *Se7en* (1995)
     (New Line Platinum Series)
     Director: David Fincher
     Label: Warner Home Video
     Release Date: 2000-12-19
     Supplements: Animated storyboards, production design.

64. *Shrek* (2001)
     (Two-Disc Special Edition)
     Directors: Andrew Adamson; Vicky Jenson
     Label: DreamWorks SKG/Universal
     Release Date: 2001-11-02
     Supplement: Storyboard pitch of deleted scenes.

65. *Signs* (2002)
     (Vista Series)
     Director: M. Night Shyamalan
     Label: Buena Vista
     Release Date: 2003-01-07
     Supplements: Storyboards: multi-angle feature.

66. **Spartacus** (1960)
(Criterion Collection)
Director: Stanley Kubrick
Label: HOME VISION
Release Date: 2001-04-24
Supplements: Original storyboards by Saul Bass; sketches by Stanley Kubrick.

67. **Star Wars: Episode I – The Phantom Menace** (1999)
(Widescreen Edition)
Director: George Lucas
Label: 20th Century Fox
Release Date: 2005-03-22
Supplements: Multi-angle storyboard to animatic to film segment featuring the submarine and Podrace Lap 1 sequences; five featurettes explore the storyline, design, costumes, visual effects, and fight sequences.

68. **Taxi Driver** (1976)
(Two-Disc Collector's Edition)
Director: Martin Scorsese
Studio: Sony Pictures
Release Date: 2007-08-14
Supplements: Storyboard to film comparisons with Martin Scorsese introduction.

69. **Tin Drum, The** (1979) (**Blechtrommel, Die**)
(Special Edition)
Director: Volker Schlöndorff
Label: Image Entertainment
Release Date: 1999-02-16
Supplements: Supplemental video section containing behind-the-scenes photos, storyboards, and more.

70. **Tomorrow Never Dies** (1997)
The James Bond Collection, Vol. 1 (Special Edition)
Director: Roger Spottiswoode
Studio: MGM (Video & DVD)
Release Date: 2002-10-22
Supplement: storyboard overlay technology that compares initial "Action-Scene" concepts with the final film.

71. ***Vertigo*** (1958)
    (Collector's Edition)
    Director: Alfred Hitchcock
    Label: Universal
    Release Date: 1998-03-31
    Supplements: Storyboards, production drawings, production photographs, and advertising materials.

72. ***Wallace and Gromit: A Grand Day Out with Wallace and Gromit*** (1989); ***Wallace & Gromit in The Wrong Trousers*** (1993); ***Wallace and Gromit in A Close Shave*** (1995); ***Wallace & Gromit: The First Three Adventures*** (1990-1995)
    Director: Nick Park
    Label: 20th Century Fox
    Release Date: 2000-06-06
    Supplements: Photo gallery and storyboards.

73. ***Wizard of Oz, The*** (1939)
    (Special Edition)
    Director: Victor Fleming
    Label: Warner Home Video
    Release Date: 1999-10-19
    Supplements: Portrait gallery, special effects stills, and stills from the Hollywood premiere; original sketches and storyboards, costume designs, and make-up tests.

STORYBOARDING / PRODUCTION DESIGN

SITES WITH WORK OF INDIVIDUAL ARTISTS

The Work of Storyboard Artist Sylvain Despretz
www.nuclearburn.com

The Work of Storyboard Artist Anthony Zierhut
www.anthonyzierhut.com

The Work of Storyboard Artist Federico D'Alessandro
www.thefilmartist.com

The Work of Storyboard Artist Richard Bennett
www.richardbennettart.com/richard.htm

The Work of Storyboard Artist Ted Boonthanakit
www.tedbstudio.com/home.html

The Work of Storyboard Artist Tim Burgard
www.timburgardart.com/storyboards.php

The Work of Storyboard Artist Rick Newsome
storyboardsinc.com/artist/newsome/newsome_film.shtml

The Work of Storyboard Artist David Hillman
www.hillmanarts.com

The Work of Storyboard Artist Adrien Van Viersen
adrienvanviersen.com

Karen J. Lloyd's Storyboard Blog
Helpful downloads and analysis of animated film sequences.
karenjlloyd.com/blog/

Richard Taylor Design Site
Storyboards, animatics, and more.
www.richardtaylordesign.com

AGENCIES THAT SPECIALIZE IN STORYBOARD ARTISTS

Famous Frames, Inc.
www.famousframes.com

Storyboards, Inc.
www.storyboardsinc.com

Frameworks Storyboard Artists LLC
www.frameworks-la.com

Giuseppe Cristiano and Marco Letizia
www.storyboardagency.com/

Storyboards Online
www.storyboardsonline.com/

OTHER SITES OF INTEREST

Star Wars Storyboards
www.swrealprops.com
theswca.com/index.php?action=disp_category&category_id=482
www.flickr.com/photos/heilemann/sets/72157594429862991/

The Bride Of Frankenstein (1935)
Description and history of the making of the film.
www.filmsite.org/bride.html

Alexandre Trauner: 50 Years of Cinema
Set designer for the likes of Welles, Wilder, and Huston.
www.lpce.com/trauner

Article on use of Storyboards for Coen Brother's films
www.myamericanartist.com/2008/05/coen-brothers-m.html

Storyboards for The Matrix
http://whatisthematrix.warnerbros.com/cmp/storyboards_index.html

Storyboard Preservation for Gone With the Wind
http://aic.stanford.edu/sg/bpg/annual/v06/bp06-10.html

COLOR AND FILM

The Technicolor Process Of Three-Color Cinematography
Text by J. A. Ball, Vice President and Technical Director, Technicolor Motion Picture Corp., Hollywood, California (Published in the *Journal of Motion Picture Engineers*, August 1935).
www.widescreenmuseum.com/oldcolor/ball.htm

Exploring the Color Image and Motion Picture Color Theory
Possibility to download some interesting publications about color. motion.
kodak.com/US/en/motion/Education/Publications/color.htm

"Art Direction: The Visual Language, Activity 3: Color and Texture"
Teacher's resource guide at www.oscars.org.
http://www.oscars.org/education-outreach/teachersguide/artdirection/activity3.html

Art direction and colors in game design
"Diablo III Producer Justifies Controversial Art Direction: 'Color is your friend'"
multiplayerblog.mtv.com/2008/07/02/diablo-iii-art-direction/

Color Psychology and Marketing
The meaning and psychology of color applied to visual communication: business, sales, and the Web.
www.precisionintermedia.com/color.html

"Color Theory," "Color Schemes," and "Psychology of Colors"
Tutorials from the Bloomsburg University of Pennsylvania, Department of Instructional Technology, Virtual Training Help Center.
iit.bloomu.edu/vthc/gd.html

The use of color on *Gangs of New York*
"Production Designer Dante Ferretti and ILM team transport viewers back to Manhattan's tumultuous past...."
www.theasc.com/magazine/jan03/mean/index.html

The look of *Surf's Up*
"In the first of a series of production diaries, production designer Paul Lasaine talks about crafting the look of Sony Pictures Animation's 3D-animated feature, *Surf's Up*."
surfsup.awn.com/?type=article&artID=2

Faber Birren — *Creative Color* text
www.questia.com/library/book/creative-color-by-faber-birren.jsp

ANIMATICS

Animatics at Creative Taco
A digital production, edit, and animation collective with over 25 years of commercial advertising experience.
www.creativetaco.com/page7/page7.html

BrainForest Digital Animatics
BrainForest is the digital animation studio that specializes in producing cutting-edge animatics.
www.brain4est.com/
See also their informational website with "everything you always wanted to know about animatics, but were afraid to ask."
www.aboutanimatics.com/

Hi Road Productions
hi road creates and delivers storyboards, animatics, comps, photomatics and live tests to a variety of advertising agencies.
www.hiroadproductions.com/

AnimaticPRO — Priceless Films
The Priceless Films Animation Studio was founded by veterans of the entertainment industry with more than thirty years of experience in games, music videos, and national television spots.
www.pricelessfilms.com/animatics.html

Animatics & Storyboards, Inc.
Character development and production animation house.
www.storyboards-east.com/about.htm

Indigo Studios Animatics
A team of artists, illustrators, photographers, 3D and video editors, and producers working for leading advertising agencies on editing, animation, and animatics.
www.indigoanimatics.com/

Continuity Studios
Neal Adams' Studios: animatics, animations, photomatics, illustrations, conceptual designs, storyboards, and cartoon storyboards.
www.nealadamsentertainment.com/

Animatics at MGV
MGV is a "can do" animatic, photomatic, and video production company for advertising agencies.
www.mgv.co.uk/web/animatics.php

Animatics Artists at *childrensillustrators.com*
A unique online community of children's illustrators.
www.childrensillustrators.com/list_animations.html?animation_category=1

Animatics at Storyboards Inc.
storyboardsinc.com/animatics.shtml

Animatics at Famous Frames
www.famousframes.com/website/animatics.php

Photoshop World Conference & Expo
Creative Storyboards and Animatics by Richard Harrington
www.photoshopforvideo.com/conferences/psworld/CreativeStoryboardsand-Animatics.pdf

VISUAL EFFECTS

Cinefex
The online guide to the ultimate in visual effects.
www.cinefex.com

CineSecrets
Insights and technical information about the making of Star Wars and other films. www.CineSecrets.com

Infinite 3D Effects Computer Animation
Computer animation, 3D animation, digital effects, 3D modeling, and the photo-real. www.infinite3dfx.com/

Industrial Video, Film TV
Animation, compositing, 3D surfacing from the Visual Effects Society.
www.visualeffectssociety.com

Visual Magic Magazine
visualmagic.awn.com

Gnomon Inc.
School of 3D Visual Effects.
www.gnomonschool.com/

"Talk like the Animals"
A look at *Dr. Dolittle's* visual effects by Ron Magid.
www.cinematographer.com/ magazine/dec98/Animals

The Making of Darth Vader's Mask
Free online museum of original movie props and costumes.
www.ketzer.com/DV_lifesized.html

Rhythm & Hues Studios
Produces animation and special effects for movies, commercials,
and television.
www.rhythm.com

Autodesk
Developer of software for digital media content creation.
usa.autodesk.com

HomeDark Horizons
Latest news on films in production (mainly dealing with blockbuster,
sci-fi, and fantasy films). A good insightful site with fan reviews and
QuickTime trailers of up-and-coming films. www.darkhorizons.com

DIRECTORS (known to have used storyboards)

The Directors Guild of America
www.dga.org

JANE CAMPION

Biographical essay
archive.sensesofcinema.com/contents/directors/02/campion.html

SERGEI EISENSTEIN

Biographical essay with links to images and video
www.videoartworld.com/beta/artist_422.html

FEDERICO FELLINI

Interview with Fellini
www.brightlightsfilm.com/26/fellini1.html

DAVID FINCHER

Conversation about and interview with David Fincher
www.thehousenextdooronline.com/2009/01/conversations-david-fincher.html
www.guardian.co.uk/film/2009/feb/03/david-fincher-interview-transcript

PETER GREENAWAY

Official site of this fascinating artist/film director
www.petergreenaway.info/

ALFRED HITCHCOCK

Alfred Hitchcock Geek
Contains a lengthy online essay and related links.
www.alfredhitchcockgeek.com/

Hitchcock Online
Includes news, book reviews and essays about Alfred Hitchcock.
www.hitchcockonline.org/

Works by or about Alfred Hitchcock
worldcat.org/identities/lccn-n79-27022

Writing with Hitchcock
www.stevenderosa.com/writingwithhitchcock/

STANLEY KUBRICK

Stanley Kubrick: The Master Filmmaker
Biography, filmography, and more
pages.prodigy.com/kubrick

The Authorized Stanley Kubrick Web Site
Warner Bros. creates the second official Kubrick-related site (mostly sells DVDs). www.kubrickfilms.com

Kubrick MultiMedia Film Guide
Images and sounds from Kubrick's works including Clockwork Orange, 2001, and Dr. Strangelove.
www.indelibleinc.com/kubrick/

The Kubrick Site
The Kubrick Site is the official Web resource of the alt.movies.kubrick news-group; it has been established as a non-profit resource archive for documentary materials regarding, in whole or in part, the work of the late American film director.
www.visual-memory.co.uk/amk

AKIRA KUROSAWA

British Film Institute (BFI) Biography page
www.bfi.org.uk/features/kurosawa/biography.html

DAVID LYNCH

Pretty as a Picture: The Art of David Lynch
80-minute documentary about the director and the making of the film *Lost Highway*.
www.finecut.com

MARTIN SCORSESE

Short bio with examples of storyboards
www.arteria.com/apetitos/2007/12/martin-scorsese-storyboards.html

ORSON WELLES

Good general site about the classic film director
www.wellesnet.com/

ROBERT WISE

"Robert Wise: American Filmmaker" on AFI.com
http://www.afi.com/wise/robert_wise.html

CINEMATOGRAPHY / CINEMATOGRAPHERS

American Society of Cinematographers
www.theasc.com/
See also their online magazine archive.
www.ascmag.com/magazine_dynamic/archive.php

The Society of Camera Operators
www.soc.org

The History of Cinematography
Comprehensive site on the development of the moving image.
www.precinemahistory.net

Steven Bradford's Electronic Cinematography
Topics include NTSC video signal, D/Vision editing, and more.
www.seanet.com/~bradford

Christopher Nibley, DP
Live action, visual effects, blue screen, and motion control cinematography. www.nibley.com

FILM REFERENCE SITES

Internet Movie Database (IMDb)
Great site for timelines and biographies of actors, directors, writers, and producers. Very basic but concise information about whomever one chooses to search for.
www.imdb.com

Women In Film Homepage
www.wif.org

America Cinema Editors
www.ace-filmeditors.org

Society of Motion Picture and Television Art Directors
www.artdirectors.org

Academy of Motion Picture Arts and Sciences
Official site for the professional organization with a special section on the annual Academy Awards.
www.oscars.org

The Official Academy Awards Site
www.oscars.com

American Movie Classics (AMC)
www.amctv.com

Britmovie
Dedicated to classic British films, cinema and movies.
www.britmovie.co.uk

The Greatest Films (AMC film site)
The greatest films in cinematic history: greatest moments, famous scenes, and film quotes. Organized by historical decades, years, and genres.
www.filmsite.org

Movie Mistakes
Large collection of continuity mistakes and film trivia.
www.movie-mistakes.com

The Criterion Collection
Continuing series of classic and contemporary films on DVD and Blu-ray editions. Features clips, art, and essays on every film in the collection.
www.criterion.com

The Film Reference Library
Online film encyclopedia and resource for Canadian and world film
http://www.filmreferencelibrary.ca/

Dreams: the Terry Gilliam Fanzine
www.smart.co.uk/dreams

The International Center for 8mm Film and Video
Cinema site for small movies.
www.littlefilm.org

Kodak
motion.kodak.com/

Giant Screen Cinema Association
Professional development network to advance the international business of producing and presenting giant screen experiences for the public.
giantscreencinema.com

The American WideScreen Museum
Widescreen systems, color history, sound development.
www.widescreenmuseum.com

American Film Institute (AFI)
National arts organization dedicated to preserving the heritage of film and television. Also houses graduate school in filmmaking, including department of production design and the Directing Workshop for Women.
www.afi.com/

The American Museum of the Moving Image
Dedicated to educating the public about the art, history, technique, and technology of film, television, and digital media, and to examining their impact on culture and society. www.movingimage.us

The British Film Institute (BFI)
The BFI is the UK's national body for film, television, and the moving image, comprising collections and archives, cinema exhibition and education. www.bfi.org.uk/

Foreignfilms
Fantastic site for the foreign film fanatic that allows one to search by film, country, or director. www.foreignfilms.com

Cyberfilmschool
A tips and tricks site for digital filmmakers (with lots of links). www.cyberfilmschool.com

LittleGoldenGuy.com
A nice reference site dedicated to all Oscar winners from 1927 to current. www.littlegoldenguy.com

Done Deal Professional: The Business and Craft of Screenwriting
A site devoted to script pitches and sales. www.donedealpro.com

Creative Screenwriting and NY Screenwriter
A site based on Creative Screenwriting magazine (loads of competitions for writers). Also archives about the magazine NY Screenwriter. www.creativescreenwriting.com

The Movie Times
Detailed site reviewing box office tallies from past to current. www.the-movie-times.com

LA 411
The bible of any L.A.-based filmmaker looking for contacts in all fields of making films. Great for sets, costumes, props, expendables, etc. www.la411.com

The Set Decorators Society of America
www.setdecorators.org

STORYBOARDS AND ARTWORK

Page

1   *Lifeboat* storyboard courtesy of the Hitchcock Estate.*

11   *The Greatest Show on Earth* storyboard courtesy of the
         Cecil B. DeMille Estate.

13   *High Anxiety* storyboard courtesy of Harold Michelson.

14   *Volcano* storyboard courtesy of Joseph Musso.

16   *Flying Brothers* storyboard courtesy of Jon Dahlstrom.

20-21   *High Anxiety* storyboard courtesy of Harold Michelson.

26   *The World According to Garp* storyboard courtesy of George Roy
         Hill.*

30-31   *The Cotton Club* storyboard courtesy of Harold Michelson.

35   *The Great Waldo Pepper* storyboard courtesy of George Roy Hill.*

39   *Monty Python and the Holy Grail* from *Gilliam on Gilliam* by Terry
         Gilliam, 1999 by Terry Gilliam. Reprinted by permission of Faber and
         Faber, an affiliate of Farrar, Strauss and Giroux, LLC.

40   *Ben-Hur* photographs courtesy of the author's collection.

42-43   *Sister, Sister* storyboard courtesy the author's collection.

47   Ron Gress interview images courtesy Digital Domain.

49   Sergei Eisenstein sketch from *Notes of a Film Director*; Foreign
         Languages Publishing House, Moscow, 1946.

52   *Vertigo* shot list with permission of the Hitchcock Estate.*

64   *North by Northwest* diagram courtesy of the Hitchcock Estate.*

71   *Lifeboat* storyboard courtesy of the Hitchcock Estate.*

81-83   Richard Taylor interview images courtesy of Electronic Arts.

97   *The Cotton Club* storyboard courtesy of Harold Michelson.

114-115 Dan Forcey interview images courtesy of Platinum Studios.

119   *Lifeboat* storyboard courtesy of the Hitchcock Estate.*

138   Steve Martino interview images courtesy of Fox Pictures/ Blue Sky
         Studios.

173   Diagram from *Conceptual Blockbusting* by James L. Adams, Perseus
         Press, 3rd ed., 1990.

209   Anton Grot sketch courtesy of UCLA Special Collections, excerpts
         from *Directing the Film* (Acrobat, 1998) used by permission.

*All images from the Hitchcock Estate and the George Roy Hill Collection held by the Margaret
Herrick Library of the Academy of Motion Picture Arts and Sciences.

FILMS

The author acknowledges the copyright owners of the following motion pictures, from which single frames have been used in this book for purposes of commentary, criticism, and scholarship under the Fair Use Doctrine.

<u>Page</u>

144   *Do the Right Thing*; Spike Lee, Director; 40 Acres and a Mule Filmworks, 1989. All Rights Reserved.

144, 165   *Matewan*; John Sayles, Director; Cinecom Entertainment Group, 1987. All Rights Reserved.

146-147, 149   *Umbrellas of Cherbourg*; Jacques Demy, Director; Parc Films, 1964. All Rights Reserved.

146-147, 162   *Far From Heaven*; Todd Haynes, Director; Focus Features, 2002. All Rights Reserved.

148, 156-157   *The Cook, the Thief, His Wife, and Her Lover*; Peter Greenaway, Director; Allarts Cook, 1989. All Rights Reserved.

148, 164   *Hero*; Zhang Yimou, Director; Miramax, 2002. All Rights Reserved.

148   *Dodes Kaden*; Akira Kurosawa, Director; Toho Company, 1970. All Rights Reserved.

149, 159   *The Last Emperor*; Bernardo Bertolucci, Director; Yanco Films Limited, 1987. All Rights Reserved.

151   *The Godfather*; Francis Ford Coppola, Director; Alfran Productions, 1972. All Rights Reserved.

152, 161   *Ran*; Akira Kurosawa, Director; Greenwich Film Productions, 1985. All Rights Reserved.

153   *Rebel Without a Cause*; Nicholas Ray, Director; Warner Bros. Pictures, 1955. All Rights Reserved.

154   *The Wizard of Oz*; Victor Fleming, Director; MGM, 1939. All Rights Reserved.

157   *Pleasantville*; Gary Ross, Director; New Line Cinema, 1998. All Rights Reserved.

160   *West Side Story*; Robert Wise; Director; MGM, 1961. All Rights Reserved.

163   *Trois Couleurs: Rouge, Bleu, Blanc*; Krzysztof Kieslowski, Director; CAB Productions, 1993–1994. All Rights Reserved.

166   *Fitzcarraldo*; Werner Hertzog, Director; Filmverlag der Autoren, 1982. All Rights Reserved.

QUOTATIONS

All quotations below that are cited as "interview" are from interviews conducted by the author in 1999 unless indicated otherwise.

Page

1   Alfred Hitchcock in Sherman, *Directing the Film*, 202.
3   George Pal in Sherman, *Directing the Film*, 98.
9   Gene Allen, interview
11   John Jensen, interview
12   King Vidor in Sherman, *Directing the Film*, 201.
14   Joseph Musso, interview
15   Richard Hoover, interview
20   Harold Michelson, interview
22   Robert Wise, interview
32   John Coven, interview
34   John Mann, interview
35   Jodi Foster, from interview on Directors Guild of America (DGA) website, accessed 1999.
38   Terry Gilliam, *Gilliam on Gilliam*, 68.
46   Ron Gress, interview.
49   Sergei Eisenstein, "Cinematographic Principle and the Ideogram," *Film Form*, 40-41.
52   Alfred Hitchcock, *Hitchcock on Hitchcock*, 186.
60   Edward Tufte, *Envisioning Information*, 9.
71   Alfred Hitchcock, *Hitchcock on Hitchcock*, 246.
74   Martin Scorsese, *Scorsese on Scorsese*, 74.
80-84   Richard Taylor, interview, 2008.
87   John Mann, interview
95, 116 John Coven, interview
109   Sergei Eisenstein, *Film Form*, 40-41.
112-116 Dan Forcey, interview, 2008.
119   Alfred Hitchcock in Bogdanovich, *Who the Devil Made It*, 38.
137-139 Steve Martino, interview, 2008.
141   Vittorio Storaro in Zone, ed., *Writer of Light: the Cinematography of Vittorio Storaro*, 53.
141   Georgia O'Keeffe, foreword to the catalogue of her exhibition, Anderson Galleries, New York, 1926.
151   Oscar Wilde in Beckson, *Oscar Wilde: The Critical Heritage*, 107.
158   Vittorio Storaro, *Writing With Light*.
164   John Sayles, *Thinking in Pictures*, 57.
167   Rudolph Arnheim, *Art and Visual Perception*, 345.
168   Vittorio Storaro in G. Brown, "Storaro and Bulworth: an Eyewitness Account of the Maestro at Work," *American Cinematographer,* v. 79, no. 6 (June 1998), 40-44.
169   Alexander Theroux, *The Primary Colors*.
171   Betty Edwards, *Drawing on the Artist Within*, 7.
193   John Huston in Sarris, ed., *Hollywood Voices*, 111.
194   Steven Spielberg in Sherman, *Directing the Film*, 98.
194   Stan Lee, *How to Draw Comics the Marvel Way*, 52.
209, 214 Phillip Mittel, interview
213   Mark Miller, interview

A SUBJECTIVE LIST OF USEFUL TEXTS

STORYBOARDS AND ART DIRECTION

By Design: Interviews With Film Designers Vincent Lobrutto; Praeger,
Westport, Conn. 1992

Drawing into Film: Director's Drawings The Pace Gallery, New York, NY, 1993 (op)

Film Architecture From Metropolis to Bladerunner Dietriech Neumann;
Prestel, Munich, Germany, 1999

Masters of Light Schaefer and Salvato; University of California Press,
Berkeley, CA, 1984

Pretty Pictures: Production Design and the History of Film C.S. Tashiro; University
of Texas Press, Austin, TX, 1998

Production Design and Art Direction Screencraft Peter Ettedgui; Focal Press,
Woburn, MA, 1999

Sets in Motion: Art Direction and Film Narrative Charles Affron and Mirella Affron;
Rutgers University Press, New Brunswick, NJ, 1995

Storyboards: Motion in Art, Third Edition Mark A. Simon; Focal Press,
Oxford, England, 2006

The Art of Hollywood: Fifty Years of Art Direction John Hambley and Patrick
Downing; Thames Television, London, England, 1979 (op)

What An Art Director Does: An Introduction to Motion Picture Production Design
Ward Preston; Focal Press, Los Angeles, CA, 1994

FILM DIRECTING

A Cut Above: 50 Film Directors Talk About Their Craft Michael Singer;
Lone Eagle, New York, NY, 1998

Art by Film Directors Karl French, Mitchell Beasley; Octopus Publishing Group,
London, England, 2004

Dark Knights and Holy Fools: The Art and Films of Terry Gilliam Bob McCabe;
Orion Publishing, London, England, 1999

Directing the Film Eric Sherman; AFI and Little, Brown & Co.,
Los Angeles, CA, 1976; reprint: Acrobat Books, Los Angeles, CA, 1988

Film Directing Fundamentals: See Your Film Before Shooting Nicholas Proferes;
Focal Press, Woburn, MA, 2008 (3rd edition)

Gilliam on Gilliam Terry Gilliam; Farber and Farber, London, England, 1999

Hitchcock on Hitchcock Sidney Gottlieb, ed.; University of California Press,
Berkeley, CA, 1997

Hitchcock/Truffaut Francois Truffaut; Simon and Schuster, New York, NY, 1983

Hollywood Voices Andrew Sarris, ed.; Bobbs-Merrill; New York, NY, 1971

Kubrick: The Definitive Edition Michel Ciment; Faber and Farber, London, England, 2004

Making Movies Work Jon Boorstin; Silman-James Press, Los Angeles, CA, 1995; Michael Singer; Lone Eagle, Los Angeles, CA, 1998

On Directing Film David Mamet; Penguin USA, New York, NY, 1992

Scorsese on Scorsese David Thompson, ed.; Farber and Farber, London, England, 1989

Something Like an Autobiography Akira Kurosawa; Vintage Books, New York, NY, 1983

The Act of Seeing Wim Wenders; Farber and Farber, London, England, 1992

The Art of Alfred Hitchcock Donald Spoto; Doubleday and Co., New York, NY, 1976

The Stanley Kubrick Archives Alison Castle; Taschen America LLC, Los Angeles, CA, 2008

The World of Peter Greenaway Leon Steinmetz, Peter Greenaway; Journey Editions, Boston, MA, 1995

Thinking in Pictures John Sayles; Houghton Mifflin, Boston, MA, 1987

Who the Devil Made It, Peter Bogdanovich; Alfred Knopf, New York, NY, 1997

THEORY/ FILM PRACTICE

Art and Visual Perception, Rudolf Arnheim; University of California Press, Berkeley, 2004 (50th Anniversary Printing)

Film Art David Bordwell and Kristen Thompson; Addison Wesley, Reading, MA, 1979

Film Directing Shot by Shot: Visualizing from Concept to Screen Steven D. Katz; Michael Wiese Productions, Los Angeles, CA, 1991

Film Form: Essays in Film Theory Sergei Eisenstein; Harcourt Brace Jovanovich, New York, NY, 1987

Grammar of the Film Language Daniel Arijon; Silman-James Press, Los Angeles, CA, 1976

Grammar of the Shot, Roy Thompson; Focal Press, Oxford, England, 1998

Hollywood Voices, Andrew Sarris, ed.; Bobbs-Merrill, New York, NY, 1971

The Five C's of Cinematography Joseph V. Mascelli; Silman-James, Los Angeles, CA, 1998

The Visual Story; Bruce Block; Focal Press, Woburn, MA, 2001

Theory of the Film Bela Balázs; Dover, New York, NY, 1970

Understanding Comics Scott McCloud; Harper Perennial, New York, NY, 1995

Writer of Light: the Cinematography of Vittorio Storaro Ray Zone, ed.; ASC Holding Corp, Los Angeles, 2001

Writing With Light, Vittorio Storaro; Aperture Books, New York, NY 2002

DRAWING

Drawing on the Artist Within, Betty Edwards; Fireside, New York, NY, 1987

Drawing on the Right Side of the Brain, Betty Edwards; J.P. Tarcher, Los Angeles, CA, 1979

How to Draw Comics the Marvel Way Stan Lee and John Buscema; Simon and Schuster, Fireside Books, New York, NY, 1978

Perspective Drawing, A Point of View Jane James; Prentice Hall, Englewood Cliffs, NJ, 1988

Perspective Drawing, An On-the-Spot Guide Mark Way; Outline Press, London, England, 1989

Perspective for Comic Book Artists David Chelsea; Watson-Guptill, New York, NY, 1997

The Natural Way to Draw Kimon Nicolaides; Houghton Mifflin Company, Boston, MA, 1969

COLOR

Color Codes: Modern Theories of Color in Philosophy, Painting and Architecture, Literature, Music, and Psychology Charles A. Riley ll; UPNE Publishing, Dartmouth, NJ, 1995

Color Psychology and Color Therapy, Faber Birren; University Books, New Hyde Park, NY, 1961

Color by Betty Edwards: A Course in Mastering the Art of Mixing Colors Betty Edwards; Tarcher Press, Los Angeles, CA, 2004

Color: A Natural History of the Palette Victoria Finlay; Random House, New York, NY, 2003

Colour – Volume 2 of Scrivere con la luce (***Writing with Light***) Vittorio Storaro;
Aperture Foundation, Accademia dell'immagine; Electa, Milan, Italy, 2001

If It's Purple, Someone's Gonna Die: The Power of Color in Visual Storytelling
Patti Bellantoni; Focal Press, Burlington, MA, 2005

Oscar Wilde: The Critical Heritage Karl E. Beckson; Routledge,
London, England (orig.); reprinted by Taylor & Francis e-Library, 2003

The Interaction of Color (**revised edition**) Joseph Albers; Yale University Press,
New Haven, CT, 2006

The Primary Colors, Three Essays Alexander Theroux; Henry Holt & Company,
New York, NY, 1996

VISUAL EFFECTS AND ANIMATION

The Animator's Survival Kit Richard Williams; Farber and Farber, London, England,
2002

*Animation Unleashed: 100 Principles Every Animator, Comic Book Writer, Film-
maker, Video Artist, and Game Developer Should Know* Ellen Besen and Bryce
Hallett; Michael Wiese Productions, Los Angeles, CA, 2008

A Century of Stop-Motion Animation: From Melies to Aardman Ray Harryhausen
and Tony Dalton; Watson-Guptill, New York, NY, 2008

Digital Storytelling: The Narrative Power of Visual Effects in Film Shilo T. McClean;
MIT Press, Boston, MA, 2008

*Directing the Story: Professional Storytelling and Storyboarding Techniques for
Live Action and Animation* Francis Glebas; Focal Press, Woburn, MA, 2008

Dream Worlds: Production Design for Animation Hans Bacher; Focal Press, Woburn,
MA 2007

Paper Dreams: The Art And Artists of Disney Storyboards John Canemaker; Disney
Editions, Los Angeles, 1999

REFERENCE

Envisioning Information Edward Tufte; Graphics Press, Cheshire, CT, 1990.

Merriam-Webster's Visual Dictionary, Merriam-Webster, Springfield, MA, 2006

The Complete Film Dictionary Ira Konigsberg; Meridian, Salinas, CA, 1987

The Macmillan Visual Dictionary Jean-Claude Corbeil, ed.; Macmillan,
New York, NY, 1994

The Story of Cinema David Shipman; St. Martin's Press, New York, NY, 1982

Ultimate Visual Dictionary, DK Publishing, New York, NY, 2006

The following pages offer generic framing examples that may be photo-copied and used for a variety of projects.

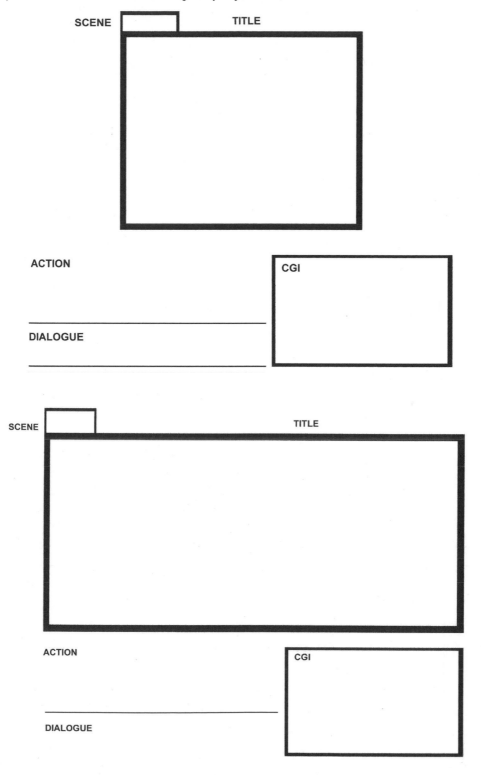

FROM WORD TO IMAGE / BEGLEITER

SCENE _____

SHOT #

ACTION

DIALOGUE

FX

SHOT #

ACTION

DIALOGUE

FX

PAGE _____

SHOT #

ACTION

DIALOGUE

FX

PAGE _____

SHOT #

ACTION
_____
_____

DIALOGUE
_____
_____

FX
_____
_____

SHOT #

ACTION
_____
_____

DIALOGUE
_____
_____

FX
_____
_____

SHOT #

ACTION
_____
_____

DIALOGUE
_____
_____

FX
_____
_____

FRAME VIEWERS

There are a number of viewfinders on the market that, without a camera, will allow you to view a scene in the appropriate aspect ratio and a variety of lens lengths. They are commonly seen around the neck of directors and cinematographers and have the appearance of a lens on a cord.

These devices often cost hundreds of dollars; while they are an excellent investment for the working professional, an alternate aid to framing up your shots can be easily and inexpensively produced using the following guides. Feel free to photocopy or cut them out of the book and make up these lightweight tools in a variety of ratios. You will find that by looking through the opening of the viewfinder, extending your arms and then pulling them slowly in, you can approximate a number of lens lengths.

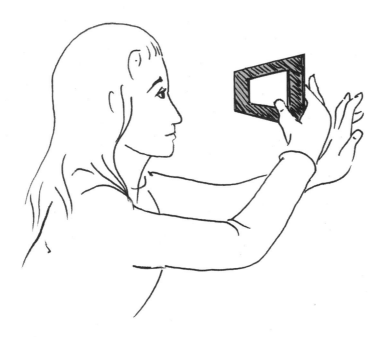

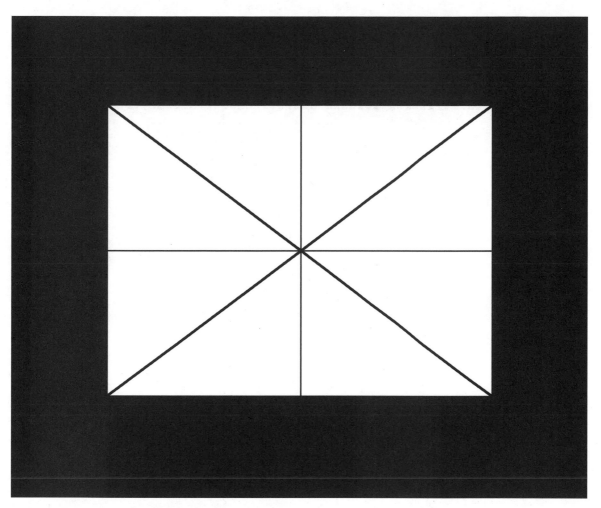

FRAME VIEWER: 1.33 ASPECT RATIO

TELEVISION AND COMPUTER MONITOR

TO USE:

> CUT OUT ON DOTTED LINES (SEE REVERSE OF SHEET)
> AFFIX TO BOARD OR FOAMCORE BASE
> TRIM BOARD TO FRAME SIZE, CUT OUT INNER BOX

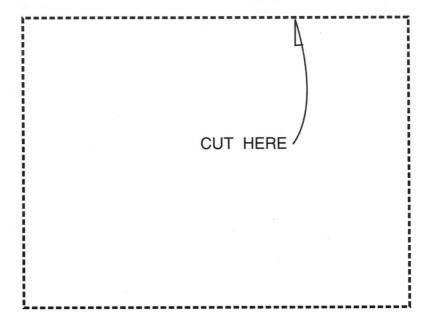

CUT HERE

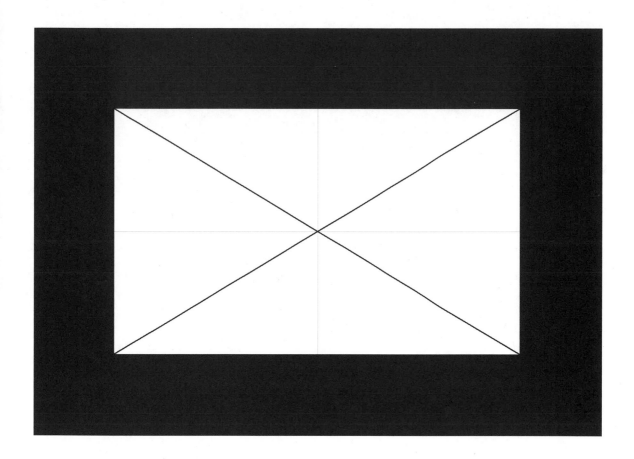

FRAME VIEWER: 1.66 ASPECT RATIO

16 MM FILM AND EUROPEAN PROJECTION

TO USE:

> CUT OUT ON DOTTED LINES (SEE REVERSE OF SHEET)
> AFFIX TO BOARD OR FOAMCORE BASE
> TRIM BOARD TO FRAME SIZE, CUT OUT INNER BOX

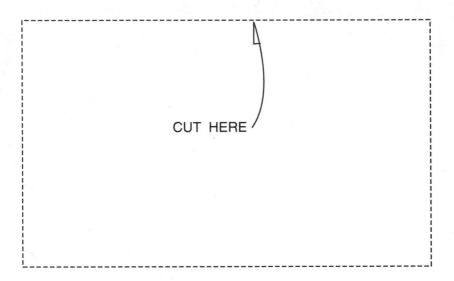

FRAME VIEWER: 1.85 ASPECT RATIO

AMERICAN PROJECTION (ACADEMY STANDARD)

TO USE:

> CUT OUT ON DOTTED LINES (SEE REVERSE OF SHEET)
> AFFIX TO BOARD OR FOAMCORE BASE
> TRIM BOARD TO FRAME SIZE, CUT OUT INNER BOX

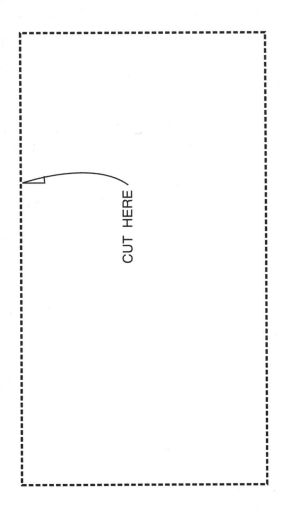

CUT HERE

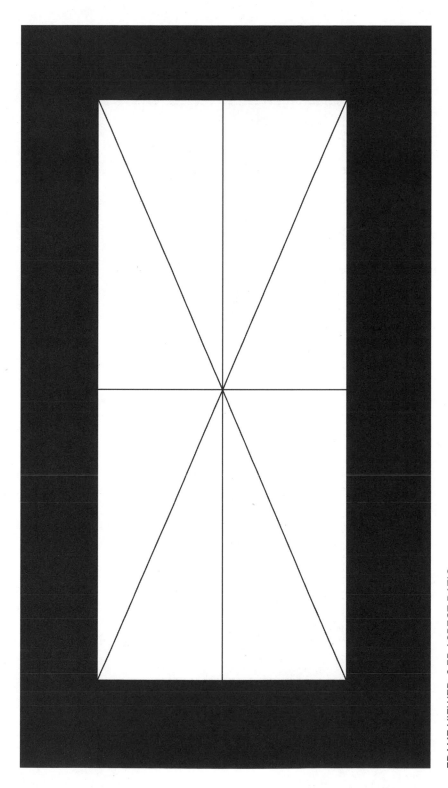

FRAME VIEWER: 2.35 ASPECT RATIO

WIDESCREEN. SUPER 35, SCOPE

TO USE:

> CUT OUT ON DOTTED LINES (SEE REVERSE OF SHEET)
> AFFIX TO BOARD OR FOAMCORE BASE
> TRIM BOARD TO FRAME SIZE, CUT OUT INNER BOX

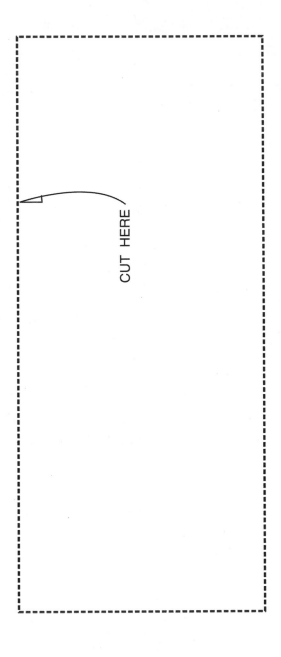

Author photo by Cary Jones

MARCIE BEGLEITER is a writer and educator who specializes in previsualization. She has worked extensively in the film, television, and interactive industries and is owner of Filmboards, whose client list includes Paramount, TriStar, New Line, HBO, and ABC. In academia, she is the founding director of the Integrated Learning Program, an interdisciplinary design curriculum, at the Otis College of Art and Design and has served on the faculties of Art Center College of Design, the American Film Institute, and the International Film School in Cologne, Germany. She has also been a featured lecturer at many venues, including the British Film Institute (BFI), the Game Developer's Conference, and the Digital Video Expo, where she has given presentations on storyboarding, color, and new media production. She is a recipient of an NEA project grant, a Foundation for Arts Resources grant, and Faculty Enrichment Grants from Art Center and Otis Colleges. In addition, Ms. Begleiter is a playwright member of the Actor's Studio.

Seminars on Storyboarding, Concept Development, and Visual Narrative can be booked through this publisher at:
info@mwp.com or at *info@marciebegleiter.com*

MASTER SHOTS
100 ADVANCED CAMERA TECHNIQUES TO GET AN EXPENSIVE LOOK ON YOUR LOW-BUDGET MOVIE

CHRISTOPHER KENWORTHY

Master Shots gives filmmakers the techniques they need to execute complex, original shots on any budget. By using powerful master shots and well-executed moves, directors can develop a strong style and stand out from the crowd. Most low-budget movies look low-budget, because the director is forced to compromise at the last minute. *Master Shots* gives you so many powerful techniques that you'll be able to respond, even under pressure, and create knock-out shots. Even when the clock is ticking and the light is fading, the techniques in this book can rescue your film, and make every shot look like it cost a fortune.

Each technique is illustrated with samples from great feature films and computer-generated diagrams for absolute clarity.

Use the secrets of the master directors to give your film the look and feel of a multi-million-dollar movie. The set-ups, moves and methods of the greats are there for the taking, whatever your budget.

"Master Shots *gives every filmmaker out there the blow-by-blow setup required to pull off even the most difficult of setups found from indies to the big Hollywood blockbusters. It's like getting all of the magician's tricks in one book."*
— Devin Watson, producer, *The Cursed*

"Though one needs to choose any addition to a film book library carefully, what with the current plethora of volumes on cinema, Master Shots *is an essential addition to any worthwhile collection."*
— Scott Essman, publisher, *Directed By* Magazine

"Christopher Kenworthy's book gives you a basic, no holds barred, no shot forgotten look at how films are made from the camera point of view. For anyone with a desire to understand how film is constructed — this book is for you."
— Matthew Terry, screenwriter/director, columnist
www.hollywoodlitsales.com

Since 2000, CHRISTOPHER KENWORTHY has written, produced, and directed drama and comedy programs, along with many hours of commercial video, tv pilots, music videos, experimental projects, and short films. He's also produced and directed over 300 visual FX shots. In 2006 he directed the web-based Australian UFO Wave, which attracted many millions of viewers. Upcoming films for Kenworthy include *The Sickness* (2009) and *Glimpse* (2011).

$24.95 · 240 PAGES · ORDER NUMBER 91RLS · ISBN: 9781932907513

24 HOURS | **1.800.833.5738** | **WWW.MWP.COM**

SETTING UP YOUR SCENES
THE INNER WORKINGS OF GREAT FILMS

RICHARD D. PEPPERMAN

Every great filmmaker has films which inspired him or her to greater and greater heights. Here, for the first time, is an awe-inspiring guide that takes you into the inner workings of classic scenes, revealing the aspects that make them great and the reasons they have served as inspirations.

An invaluable resource for screenwriter, cinematographer, actor, director, and editor, Pepperman's book uses examples from six decades of international films to illustrate what happens when story, character, dialogue, text, subtext, and set-ups come together to create cinematic magic.

With over 400 photos of selected movie clips laid out beautifully in a widescreen format, this book shows you how to emulate the masters and achieve your dreams.

"Setting Up Your Scenes *is both visually stunning and very useful for students of cinema. Its design, layout, and content make the book unique and irresistible.*"
 – Amresh Sinha, New York University/The School of Visual Arts

"*Pepperman has written a book which should form the basis for an intelligent discussion about the basic building blocks of great scenes across a wide variety of films. Armed with the information in this book, teachers, students, filmmakers, and film lovers can begin to understand how good editing and scene construction can bring out the best storytelling to create a better film.*"
 – Norman Hollyn, Associate Professor and Editing Track Head,
   School of Cinema-Television at the University of Southern California

"*Pepperman dissects some very infamous scenes from some very famous movies — providing us with the most breathtaking black and white stills — in order to highlight the importance of the interplay between dialogue, subtext, and shot selection in great filmmaking.*"
 – Lily Sadri, Writer, Screenwriter, *Fixing Fairchild*,
   Contributor to *www.absolutewrite.com*

RICHARD D. PEPPERMAN has been a film editor for more than 40 years and a teacher for more than 30. He is the author of *The Eye Is Quicker*.

$24.95 · 245 PAGES · ORDER NUMBER 42RLS · ISBN: 1932907084

CINEMATIC STORYTELLING
THE 100 MOST POWERFUL FILM CONVENTIONS EVERY FILMMAKER MUST KNOW

JENNIFER VAN SIJLL

BEST SELLER

How do directors use screen direction to suggest conflict? How do screenwriters exploit film space to show change? How does editing style determine emotional response?

Many first-time writers and directors do not ask these questions. They forego the huge creative resource of the film medium, defaulting to dialog to tell their screen story. Yet most movies are carried by sound and picture. The industry's most successful writers and directors have mastered the cinematic conventions specific to the medium. They have harnessed non-dialog techniques to create some of the most cinematic moments in movie history.

This book is intended to help writers and directors more fully exploit the medium's inherent storytelling devices. It contains 100 non-dialog techniques that have been used by the industry's top writers and directors. From *Metropolis* and *Citizen Kane* to *Dead Man* and *Kill Bill*, the book illustrates — through 500 frame grabs and 75 script excerpts — how the inherent storytelling devices specific to film were exploited.

You will learn:
 · How non-dialog film techniques can advance story.
 · How master screenwriters exploit cinematic conventions to create powerful scenarios.

"Cinematic Storytelling *scores a direct hit in terms of concise information and perfectly chosen visuals, and it also searches out... and finds... an emotional core that many books of this nature either miss or are afraid of.*"
> – Kirsten Sheridan, Director, *Disco Pigs*; Co-writer, *In America*

"*Here is a uniquely fresh, accessible, and truly original contribution to the field. Jennifer van Sijll takes her readers in a wholly new direction, integrating aspects of screenwriting with all the film crafts in a way I've never before seen. It is essential reading not only for screenwriters but also for filmmakers of every stripe.*"
> – Prof. Richard Walter, UCLA Screenwriting Chairman

JENNIFER VAN SIJLL has taught film production, film history, and screenwriting. She is currently on the faculty at San Francisco State's Department of Cinema.

$24.95 · 230 PAGES · ORDER NUMBER 35RLS · ISBN: 9781932907056

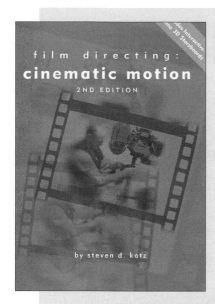

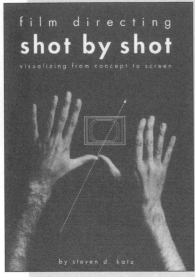

FILM DIRECTING: SHOT BY SHOT
VISUALIZING FROM CONCEPT TO SCREEN

STEVEN D. KATZ

BEST SELLER
OVER 200,000 COPIES SOLD!

Film Directing: Shot by Shot — with its famous blue cover — is the best-known book on directing and a favorite of professional directors as an on-set quick reference guide.

This international bestseller is a complete catalog of visual techniques and their stylistic implications, enabling working filmmakers to expand their knowledge.

Contains in-depth information on shot composition, staging sequences, visualization tools, framing and composition techniques, camera movement, blocking tracking shots, script analysis, and much more.

Includes over 750 storyboards and illustrations, with never-before-published storyboards from Steven Spielberg's *Empire of the Sun*, Orson Welles' *Citizen Kane*, and Alfred Hitchcock's *The Birds*.

"(To become a director) you have to teach yourself what makes movies good and what makes them bad. John Singleton has been my mentor... he's the one who told me what movies to watch and to read Shot by Shot."
> — Ice Cube, *New York Times*

"A generous number of photos and superb illustrations accompany each concept, many of the graphics being from Katz' own pen... Film Directing: Shot by Shot *is a feast for the eyes."*
> — *Videomaker* Magazine

"... demonstrates the visual techniques of filmmaking by defining the process whereby the director converts storyboards into photographed scenes."
> — *Back Stage Shoot*

"Contains an encyclopedic wealth of information."
> — *Millimeter* Magazine

STEVEN D. KATZ is an award-winning filmmaker and also the author of *Film Directing: Cinematic Motion*.

$27.95 · 366 PAGES · ORDER NUMBER 7RLS · ISBN: 9780941188104

{ THE MYTH OF MWP }

In a dark time, a light bringer came along, leading the curious and the frustrated to clarity and empowerment. It took the well-guarded secrets out of the hands of the few and made them available to all. It spread a spirit of openness and creative freedom, and built a storehouse of knowledge dedicated to the betterment of the arts.

The essence of the Michael Wiese Productions (MWP) is empowering people who have the burning desire to express themselves creatively. We help them realize their dreams by putting the tools in their hands. We demystify the sometimes secretive worlds of screenwriting, directing, acting, producing, film financing, and other media crafts.

By doing so, we hope to bring forth a realization of 'conscious media' which we define as being positively charged, emphasizing hope and affirming positive values like trust, cooperation, self-empowerment, freedom, and love. Grounded in the deep roots of myth, it aims to be healing both for those who make the art and those who encounter it. It hopes to be transformative for people, opening doors to new possibilities and pulling back veils to reveal hidden worlds.

MWP has built a storehouse of knowledge unequaled in the world, for no other publisher has so many titles on the media arts. Please visit www.mwp.com where you will find many free resources and a 25% discount on our books. Sign up and become part of the wider creative community!

Onward and upward,

Michael Wiese
Publisher/Filmmaker

FILM & VIDEO BOOKS

TO RECEIVE A FREE MWP NEWSLETTER, CLICK ON WWW.MWP.COM TO REGISTER

SCREENWRITING | WRITING

And the Best Screenplay Goes to... | Dr. Linda Seger | $26.95

Archetypes for Writers | Jennifer Van Bergen | $22.95

Cinematic Storytelling | Jennifer Van Sijll | $24.95

Could It Be a Movie? | Christina Hamlett | $26.95

Creating Characters | Marisa D'Vari | $26.95

Crime Writer's Reference Guide, The | Martin Roth | $20.95

Deep Cinema | Mary Trainor-Brigham | $19.95

Elephant Bucks | Sheldon Bull | $24.95

Fast, Cheap & Written That Way | John Gaspard | $26.95

Hollywood Standard, The | Christopher Riley | $18.95

I Could've Written a Better Movie than That! | Derek Rydall | $26.95

Inner Drives | Pamela Jaye Smith | $26.95

Joe Leydon's Guide to Essential Movies You Must See | Joe Leydon | $24.95

Moral Premise, The | Stanley D. Williams, Ph.D. | $24.95

Myth and the Movies | Stuart Voytilla | $26.95

Power of the Dark Side, The | Pamela Jaye Smith | $22.95

Psychology for Screenwriters | William Indick, Ph.D. | $26.95

Rewrite | Paul Chitlik | $16.95

Romancing the A-List | Christopher Keane | $18.95

Save the Cat! | Blake Snyder | $19.95

Save the Cat! Goes to the Movies | Blake Snyder | $24.95

Screenwriting 101 | Neill D. Hicks | $16.95

Screenwriting for Teens | Christina Hamlett | $18.95

Script-Selling Game, The | Kathie Fong Yoneda | $16.95

Stealing Fire From the Gods, 2nd Edition | James Bonnet | $26.95

Way of Story, The | Catherine Ann Jones | $22.95

What Are You Laughing At? | Brad Schreiber | $19.95

Writer's Journey, – 3rd Edition, The | Christopher Vogler | $26.95

Writer's Partner, The | Martin Roth | $24.95

Writing the Action Adventure Film | Neill D. Hicks | $14.95

Writing the Comedy Film | Stuart Voytilla & Scott Petri | $14.95

Writing the Killer Treatment | Michael Halperin | $14.95

Writing the Second Act | Michael Halperin | $19.95

Writing the Thriller Film | Neill D. Hicks | $14.95

Writing the TV Drama Series – 2nd Edition | Pamela Douglas | $26.95

Your Screenplay Sucks! | William M. Akers | $19.95

FILMMAKING

Film School | Richard D. Pepperman | $24.95

Power of Film, The | Howard Suber | $27.95

PITCHING

Perfect Pitch – 2nd Edition, The | Ken Rotcop | $19.95

Selling Your Story in 60 Seconds | Michael Hauge | $12.95

SHORTS

Filmmaking for Teens | Troy Lanier & Clay Nichols | $18.95

Ultimate Filmmaker's Guide to Short Films, The | Kim Adelman | $16.95

BUDGET | PRODUCTION MGMT

Film & Video Budgets, 4th Updated Edition | Deke Simon & Michael Wiese | $26.95

Film Production Management 101 | Deborah S. Patz | $39.95

DIRECTING | VISUALIZATION

Animation Unleashed | Ellen Besen | $26.95

Citizen Kane Crash Course in Cinematography | David Worth | $19.95

Directing Actors | Judith Weston | $26.95

Directing Feature Films | Mark Travis | $26.95

Fast, Cheap & Under Control | John Gaspard | $26.95

Film Directing: Cinematic Motion, 2nd Edition | Steven D. Katz | $27.95

Film Directing: Shot by Shot | Steven D. Katz | $27.95

Film Director's Intuition, The | Judith Weston | $26.95

First Time Director | Gil Bettman | $27.95

From Word to Image | Marcie Begleiter | $26.95

I'll Be in My Trailer! | John Badham & Craig Modderno | $26.95

Master Shots | Christopher Kenworthy | $24.95

Setting Up Your Scenes | Richard D. Pepperman | $24.95

Setting Up Your Shots, 2nd Edition | Jeremy Vineyard | $22.95

Working Director, The | Charles Wilkinson | $22.95

DIGITAL | DOCUMENTARY | SPECIAL

Digital Filmmaking 101, 2nd Edition | Dale Newton & John Gaspard | $26.95

Digital Moviemaking 3.0 | Scott Billups | $24.95

Digital Video Secrets | Tony Levelle | $26.95

Greenscreen Made Easy | Jeremy Hanke & Michele Yamazaki | $19.95

Producing with Passion | Dorothy Fadiman & Tony Levelle | $22.95

Special Effects | Michael Slone | $31.95

EDITING

Cut by Cut | Gael Chandler | $35.95

Cut to the Chase | Bobbie O'Steen | $24.95

Eye is Quicker, The | Richard D. Pepperman | $27.95

Invisible Cut, The | Bobbie O'Steen | $28.95

SOUND | DVD | CAREER

Complete DVD Book, The | Chris Gore & Paul J. Salamoff | $26.95

Costume Design 101 | Richard La Motte | $19.95

Hitting Your Mark – 2nd Edition | Steve Carlson | $22.95

Sound Design | David Sonnenschein | $19.95

Sound Effects Bible, The | Ric Viers | $26.95

Storyboarding 101 | James Fraioli | $19.95

There's No Business Like Soul Business | Derek Rydall | $22.95

FINANCE | MARKETING | FUNDING

Art of Film Funding, The | Carole Lee Dean | $26.95

Complete Independent Movie Marketing Handbook, The | Mark Steven Bosko | $39.95

Independent Film and Videomakers Guide – 2nd Edition, The | Michael Wiese | $29.95

Independent Film Distribution | Phil Hall | $26.95

Shaking the Money Tree, 2nd Edition | Morrie Warshawski | $26.95

OUR FILMS

Dolphin Adventures: DVD | Michael Wiese and Hardy Jones | $24.95

On the Edge of a Dream | Michael Wiese | $16.95

Sacred Sites of the Dalai Lamas– DVD, The | Documentary by Michael Wiese | $24.95

Hardware Wars: DVD | Written and Directed by Ernie Fosselius | $14.95

To Order go to *www.mwp.com* or Call 1-800-833-5738